H O R I Z
STUDIES IN LITE
General Editor: Penn

Early Poetry of T. S. Eliot

Robin Grove
Senior Lecturer in English
University of Melbourne

SYDNEY
UNIVERSITY PRESS

SYDNEY UNIVERSITY PRESS
in association with
OXFORD UNIVERSITY PRESS AUSTRALIA

First published 1993

National Library of Australia
Cataloguing-in-Publication data:

Grove, Robin
Early poetry of T. S. Eliot.

ISBN 0 424 00193 4.

1. Eliot, T. S. (Thomas (Stearns), 1888–1965—Criticism and interpretation. I. Title. (Series: Horizon studies in literature).

821 912

Cover illustration by Jiri Tibor Novak
Typeset by Solo Typesetting, South Australia
Printed and bound by The Book Printer, Victoria
Published by Sydney University Press in association
with Oxford University Press,
253 Normanby Road, South Melbourne, Australia

FOREWORD

More often than not, set texts for high school and undergraduate students seems overly familiar: the reader's relationship with them is tired. Although it is probably true that all authors hope their work will become 'classics', they would never intend them to become tiresomely familiar. The aim of this series of short criticial studies is to refresh students' and teachers' reading of these books, by offering detailed close analysis allied to an overview informed by recent trends in criticism and scholarship.

Literary criticism is never static; what seems important to say about a work twenty or fifty years ago will seem glaringly obvious, or irrelevant, to us today. This is because our own perspective or way of viewing the world limits and defines our reading, especially our reading of the past (even the recent past). The critical endeavour should be to make our 'horizon' meet the horizon of the work, the author's world. Neither cancels out the other, but what the work 'says' to us depends on the questions that we think are relevant to ask about it. The text remains a classic because modern readers can gain both meaning and pleasure from their reading of it.

It is hoped that students will find these studies liberating, by encouraging them to ask new questions of their set texts, in providing them with new information about the writer's world (both historical and imaginative), and in directing them to techniques of critical reading that they may not yet have encountered. The ultimate aim of this series is to expand the reader's horizon.

Penny Gay
English Department, University of Sydney

CONTENTS

PREFACE

For Elisabeth

Poetry, like other writing, needs to be carefully read. A difficulty in the case of Eliot's verse is that no edition of the poems prints them without errors or ambiguities of punctuation and lay-out. The text used in this essay is that of the *Complete Poems and Plays* (London: Faber, 1969) but altered where necessary to bring it into line with printings which for one reason or another seem better.

Rather than clutter discussion with footnotes, I have supplemented the text only when information about sources, further examples, and various kinds of additional material seemed immediately helpful. I have also written as if the reader will always have a copy of the poems open as they read. Consequently, the discussion assumes the *whole* of any poem is available, even when only a portion is quoted.

Knowing how difficult the poetry can seem, I have been happy to believe that the reader will make constant use of such aids as B. C. Southam's *A Student's Guide to the Selected Poems of T. S. Eliot*, and Valerie Eliot's facsimile and transcripts of the *Waste Land* drafts, as well as the Notes to the latter poem provided by Eliot himself.

The section headings are derived from the following poems which, read in sequence, provide a sort of X-ray of interests and preoccupations in Eliot's verse-writing:

lunar incantations ('Rhapsody on a Windy Night' 1. 4)
Along the reaches of the street ('Rhapsody on a Windy Night' 1. 2)
a gesture and a pose ('La Figlia Che Piange' 1. 22)
Follow the dance/Of the goldfinch at noon ('Cape Ann' ('Landscapes') 1. 3–4)
Come under the shadow of this gray rock ('The Death of Saint Narcissus' 1. 1)
The smoky candle-end of time/Declines ('Burbank with a Baedeker: Bleistein with a cigar' 1. 20)
Shall these bones live? shall these/Bones live? (Ash-Wednesday II. 1. 5–6)
Entering the whirlpool (The Waste Land IV. 1. 318)
But the fountain sprang up and the bird sang down (Ash-Wednesday IV. 1. 25)
Where is the end of them . . .? ('The Dry Salvages' II 1. 19)

Penny Gay, who first suggested the project, has been the best of editors. Without the stimulus of David Moody's work on Eliot, and his friendship, generously active for many years, there would have been no such book as this. Vincent Buckley, S. L. Goldberg, and Maggie Tomlinson are present throughout, most vividly perhaps where I know they would have disagreed. Helen Dell helped with Eliot's music, and not just in practical ways. But my greatest debt is recorded at the start of this Preface.

I

MAKING IT ALL UP

My words echo
Thus, in your mind.

The words just quoted can be found in T. S. Eliot's *Collected Poems*. These particular words in fact come early in 'Burnt Norton', a poem of 1935, and not only do they draw attention to themselves, they sound as if they are rather pointedly directed our way—aimed at the reader, that is. It is a rare thing to be buttonholed so abruptly by a phrase which stares straight at you, and yet looks forward to arriving on the other side of the present, where it will continue with you even after it has passed. Such writing has an unsettling effect, like something that issues in broad daylight out of a haunted house.

Perhaps appropriately, therefore, none of its details can easily be laid to rest. The first line speaks of 'My' words, but who exactly is saying them? The poet? It is tempting to suppose so, but no such figure has entered the verse. If we must identify a speaker here, we might do better to imagine the poem itself turning suddenly to address its reader, 'My words echo/Thus, in your mind': not an author communicating with us, but the poem's own words on the page. And sure enough, the echo indicated 'Thus' turns out to be the repeat of another imaginary noise conjured up by the sentence before:

Footfalls echo in the memory,
Down the passage which we did not take
Towards the door we never opened
Into the rose-garden.

But this is more and more eerie, for if we just had a poem speaking up for itself, now what we get is a memory of something that *didn't* happen. There was (says the verse) no opened door, no passage we walked down, no footsteps. So how can such things be recalled? Just where clarity might have emerged, we find it escapes us again, in the twists of a writing dedicated to denying the very actions it performs.

They never actually took place; and yet they did. Because 'echo' is just what these purely verbal footsteps do. Footfalls do echo in the memory, when one word (down-up) thus mimics the pattern of the other, the sound's two syllables sounding again—*footfall, echo*—exactly as the verse said they would. It is a happening alright, but entirely made out of words. Similarly, we might observe how the 'passage' which we did not take becomes the passage we are reading here and now, while its apparent dead-end, at 'the door we never opened', turns instead to a new perspective as, on the hinge of the line, something does give way, opening as the phrase says 'Into the rose-garden', against the resistance of plain sense, whose syntax declares that the unopened door stayed shut.

At every point, then, the poetry creates imaginary events and simultaneously cancels them out. It is not inviting us into an imitation of the 'real' world, but into a drama taking place in language itself, where words perform the only actions that there are. And this curious effect gives a point of entry into Eliot's work as a writer.

lunar incantations

For a long time, critics objected to Eliot's apparent remoteness from what they supposed a poet should be like. At certain moments intimidatingly intellectual (witness the notorious Notes appended to *The Waste Land*), at others he seemed unheroic if not downright silly.

I grow old . . . I grow old . . .
I shall wear the bottoms of my trousers rolled.

It was hard even to decide what he meant by that second line: is it modestly unpretentious to roll up one's trouser-cuffs, a puzzled reader in the 1950s wanted to know, or are we to think of it as the defeated gesture of a futile seedy life? Debate, obviously, on such a point might go this way or that; but few commentators thought to notice that the trousers had been rolled in order to rhyme, grandly, with the line that went before. Reading 'Prufrock', they assumed they were dealing with a person, whereas what they were actually confronted by was a poem.[1]

Similarly with the critic (Edmund Wilson, in *Axel's Castle*, 1931) who complained he was tired of hearing Eliot, 'only in his early forties, present himself as an "agèd eagle" who asks why he should stretch his wings'; or the even more disconcerted reviewer affronted by what he took to be the poet's ambition to become a crab. None of these protestors assumed that verse-writing might have any other effect than to communicate a philosophy-of-life and provide a platform for the author's own self-expression.

For the time being, however, let us suppose that the author is not our business, and neither is that concoction out of the idea of Author: the idea of characters 'he' has made. Prufrock is simply a word. Not a name—that already lets in the idea that Prufrock may be a personality, and we are conjecturing that the pages of a book do not contain people, only words—but in the case of 'Prufrock' a wonderfully evocative word, resonant with possibility, so that inside the syllables first one suggestion then another—*prudent, prudish*, even *prurient*, with its shame-faced sexual interest—half-rears its head, only to combine contradictorily with the high moral overtones of Victorian *frock-coats*, or the even higher overtones of the same period's business standards (*proof* against anything, *rock-solid*) and its hymns ('*Rock of Ages*'). The effect grows richer still when to all this is added the prim self-satisfaction of 'J. Alfred', and the erotic yearning implied by 'Love Song'. Put the six words together, and the title becomes a miniature poem in itself.

It is followed immediately by another, this time in a foreign tongue, as a soul from Dante's *Inferno* (xxvii. 61-6) claims the right to speak.

> S'io credessi che mia risposta fosse . . .[2]

But even before looking up the source of these phrases (they come from one of the deceitful counsellors in Hell), their very foreignness throws into doubt the seemingly confident turn of phrase with which the English language takes over from where the Italian died away: 'Let us go then, you and I'. The transition from one culture, one world, to another surely can't be as straightforward as that. Dante's speaker was trapped, indeed, in a torment of self-knowledge from which there could never be escape, so how warily might we need to negotiate this Love-Song which opens with a warning that from the gulf of false counsel no one ever returns alive? American, medieval, commercial, visionary: the poem of 1909 takes its rise somewhere inside echo-chambers where other times and other places have put words together; and its 'you' and 'I' are not familiar entities, but—like everything on the page—enigmas, written signs awaiting interpretation.

No certainty, therefore, can tell us the opening lines are spoken by Prufrock to an unnamed companion. Such a scenario might have its place in a narrative or a drama, but not here. On the contrary, this non-story-telling poem is so constructed as to separate the Prufrock of its title from whatever poetry might follow, for not only does it begin with lines which certainly aren't his ('*S'io credessi che mai risposta fosse* . . .'), but it denaturalizes its scenery in the very act of evoking time and place. Evening is spread out 'Like a patient'; something is up for investigation, one must feel. And if the reader looks again, allowing naturalistic expectations to drop away, the 'I', 'you', 'us' encountered in these opening phrases turn out to be *grammatical* figures—pieces of writing—before they are anything else. They are words, words which within a couple of lines, it is proposed, are passing through half-deserted places (and true enough, the scene is virtually empty of characters of any kind). Not people, but pronouns, they pass 'through' streets, the poem says, and that is accurate too, since the streets traversed and left behind (line 4) turn up again further along (line 8), this time openly pursuing the reader:

> Streets that follow like a tedious argument
> Of insidious intent
> To lead you to an overwhelming question . . .

Usually, an argument is something you try to follow; here, the argument follows *you*, yet at the same time is leading you on. Or at any rate the argument-like street is doing so. There is no actual argument advanced: like everything else in the paragraph—actors, evening, sky—it is nothing more than a word. Except that, inside a poem, to be a word is precisely to have power. So the verse does what it says: the streets do move around us, as they follow and simultaneously precede, coming before and behind, and re-emerging through the interrupted grammar even while the sentence is still taking us away from their first appearance. There is no getting outside the involutions of the writing, which even forestalls our questions ('Oh, do not ask, "What is it?"') by letting it be felt that such questions would themselves forestall the far greater question (as uncapturable as the 'argument') the poetry has up its sleeve.

These are strange metamorphoses of the mind. To turn thinking inside out, and entangle the reader in the act of reading, so that language itself points beyond the world of sense, is part of what the Symboliste strain in Eliot's Modernism aimed to do. We don't help ourselves, therefore, if we think of the Love-Song as a dramatic monologue, in the style of Browning perhaps. Such a term (and many critics have used it) encourages the reader to expect an incipient story and search out a single speaker or a 'character' with a point of view. Even so adventurous an analyst as Hugh Kenner (*The Invisible Poet* [1964], p. 40) talks of Prufrock as a possible zone of consciousness; but that, which would describe the illusion Browning creates with the Duke in 'My Last Duchess', seems far from the weird music Eliot's poem sings. I'm not even sure that our calling it 'Eliot's poem' does much good, since what the phrase implies is that the poem belongs to an author who is (and ought to be) in control, shaping the verse according to intention, whereas we seem to find in 'Prufrock' a less autonomous, less ego-centred process than that. The writing gives the effect of composing *itself*, rather than obeying the conscious decisions of the writer's will, as when the lines set up a rhythmical onwardness—

Let us go then, you and I,
When the evening is spread out against the sky
Like a patient etherised upon a table;
Let us go, through certain half-deserted streets,
The muttering retreats
Of restless nights in one-night cheap hotels
And sawdust restaurants with oyster-shells

—within whose impulsions the rhyming draws the writing forward to discover, and then inventively play upon, word after word, phrase after phrase. *Streets* become *retreats*, and on the further side of their hotels nothing remains but that exactly fitting discard, *oyster-shells*. Out of such chimes and echoes and verbal to-and-fro the whole edifice is made. Solid therefore as the scene appears with all its detail, it is palpably nothing but language; and language moreover which constructs unvisualizable moments of text, since along what streets could any walker go where restless nights have hidden themselves in mutterings, and restaurants are summoned up as 'sawdust' only? There is of course no city, no picturable urban scene, only the leading and the following of the poetry—for the Prufrock locales are about as substantial as a hologram, where the illusion of substance arises just from light intersecting with itself in a pattern of specialized effects.

It is the same among the smoke and fog of that December afternoon where 'Portrait of a Lady''s darkened room has hardly even begun to shape itself before it is being dissolved:

> You have the scene arrange itself—as it will seem to do—

unsubstantiated by the very 'you' or eye that sees it. Who exactly is responsible for the stage-management, though? That first pronoun could apply to the lady, to the young man addressing himself, or to you, reader, as you read on here and now. Perhaps all three are entangled in the line. Yet maybe not, if there was only the scene arranging *itself*—a possibility further decertainized by the succeeding phrase, 'as it will seem to do'. To whom, we might wonder, will it look as if it's doing that? 'You have the scene arrange itself': impossible by now to assign any of the actors, ourselves included, a clear fixed place. Indeed, we can see already that the setting itself is just as much a participant in the unfolding drama as any of its human figures.

For everything in this language-world is an ongoing composition; not a series of solidities carefully described, but a set of variations rather as in music, so that *room* by its very sound will precipitate *Juliet's tomb*, just as later it will touch against that *bloom* which concert-goers merely rub and question, or be found still later again in the vicinity of lilacs ('Now that lilacs are in bloom'), one phrase conjuring another, then another. The scenery is all music and atmospherics in this darkened place whose walls, rising from the smoke and fog of the fading day, turn out to be no more solid than the rings of light upon the ceiling overhead. In much this fashion throughout the poem light simultaneously reveals and unmakes, as it gathers itself into afternoons grey and smoky, evenings yellow and rose, while smoke and dust fill the skyline, and the natural world drifts toward oblivion or hangs in a tobacco trance. The soft disintegration of the landscape, with its diffusions and refractions, its laden air, makes it harder than ever to find a secure footing, since voices and unspoken thoughts replace action almost entirely, and the setting is scarcely solid enough to bear the weight of a gesture.

But the triumph of 'Portrait of a Lady', it seems to me, is not in sensuous effects themselves, so much as in the crisis of bewilderment, anguish, panic, precipitated by a world always threatening to dissolve into unreality. Even in 'Prufrock' we are carried beyond social fears and vacillations—beyond the imagined embarrassments of eyes fixing on details of dress, towards the disturbing suspicion that the self itself ('And how should I begin? . . . Shall I say . . . I should have been a pair of ragged claws . . .') might be no more than a series of roles parading round a void. How much more painful, then, the idea becomes in 'Portrait of a Lady', where every gesture seems a falsity, yet the actors, the setting, even the seasons, are trapped inside their own performance, never able to escape their parts.

So tea is served, as always, and the latest Pole transmits the Preludes; the lilacs arrive in April, the October night comes down in its old remembered way, to be met by the man returning 'as before'; the very conversation is a turning and returning upon itself: '"And how, how rare and strange it is to find . . . To find a friend . . ."'. Everything is already a repeat. It is not hard to mock at such artificial flowers. Adept, however, at detecting the 'false note' in what the woman so painfully and theatrically composes as conversation, the young man of the poem strikes a pose of indifference which is quite as hard to take. Her over-intimacy of manner is cruelly answered by his callow would-be detachment. But can we find a footing for *our* imaginative behaviour in responding to the pressures of the scene? That is the challenge of the poem. We may begin by shrinking from the lady, but before long the young man's manner begins to seem no less presumptuous and jarring on the nerves. Yet what if our detachment from him is just a different version of his own fastidious-brutal refusal of sympathy? If so, even in objecting to the crudely dismissive rhymes with which he turns away ('Correct our watches by the public clocks./Then sit for half an hour and drink our bocks'), the reader is thoroughly implicated. We are shown what it is to look with a judging eye; in the world of this poem, you could almost literally *see through* everything, but where does that leave the consciousness that chooses to do so? The difficulty of being open and sensitive enough to the demands of these demanding voices is poignantly brought home in the undoing of the speaker

> when a street-piano, mechanical and tired
> Reiterates some worn-out common song
> With the smell of hyacinths across the garden
> Recalling things that other people have desired.
> Are these ideas right or wrong?

and the even more uncertain poignancy with which the drama ends:

> Well! and what if she should die some afternoon . . .
> Should die and leave me sitting pen in hand
> With the smoke coming down above the housetops;
> Doubtful, for a while
> Not knowing what to feel or if I understand
> Or whether wise or foolish, tardy or too soon . . .
> Would she not have the advantage, after all?
> This music is successful with a 'dying fall'
> Now that we talk of dying—
> And should I have the right to smile?

It is a melancholy ending—for this fictional young man, as well as for the woman he recollects. And the saddest touch of all is that the speaker, pen in hand, can think of himself as doubtful only 'for a while': his moment of uncertainty lasting so short a time. For no sooner does he start to dramatize his incapacity—'Not knowing what to feel', etc.—than reassuringly eloquent phrases fill the gap, 'wise . . . foolish . . . tardy or too soon'. Not just eloquence, either, but fears too are ready to hand: 'Would she not have the advantage, after all?' Yet the final question breaks through it all—breaks through the nervousness, the self-congratulation, the careful literary reminiscence of *Twelfth Night*'s 'dying fall'; supplants the cultivated manner, and remains to haunt the reader: 'And should I have the right to smile?' That is where we end the poem, on a troubling note of interrogation, applied as much to ourselves as to the Portrait's self-inspecting, self-doubting 'I'.

Along the reaches of the street

Prufrock and Other Observations: the title chosen for Eliot's first published volume has such a decidedly clinical air, it can sound off-putting even today. Plenty of readers have felt that its twelve poems lack sympathy all round; and many of them do, or seem to, at least; but this detachment itself may need a second look—as with the situation just considered. Similarly in 'Morning at the Window', another poem in which the observer is observed. Here, the watcher finds nothing but pointlessness in the scene surveyed. The sea of fog tosses up distorted faces, aimless evaporating smiles. The street with its trampled edges is worn out; even souls can do no more than sprout despondently. But it is left for the reader to diagnose the malaise, that withering class-superiority which, confronted by the working life of a household, registers nothing but distance: 'They' [nameless creatures]

> are rattling breakfast plates in basement kitchens

Mechanical arms, or large hungry mice, might do the same. One's servants can't be regarded as human, after all, even if food and comfort depend on their daily efforts. And similarly in establishments further down the street where one's well-to-do neighbours live: 'I am aware' [how graciously condescending, that the mind should bend so low]

> I am aware of the damp souls of housemaids
> Sprouting despondently at area gates.

We will never know what the housemaids themselves might be aware of, what consciousness of their employers they enjoy, since vegetables don't rise so high. Their morning is merely fatigued, like everything else in the poem. No wonder that for this observer, glassily sealed off behind the window, nothing is left in the end: the one possibility glimpsed of human interaction, a smile, hovers directionless a moment, then vanishes 'along the level of the roofs'.

Failed connections, then, might be said to be all that is holding these random items together: what comes under scrutiny in this characteristic piece of the *Prufrock* volume is the patronizingly satiric 'observing' mode itself. Or one might take a simpler, sharper example still: such as 'Aunt Helen', where, neatly managed as the comedy is, it is so determined to keep disturbance at a distance that it actually witnesses to the disturbing force of those possibilities it is being ironical about.

Miss Helen Slingsby was my maiden aunt,
And lived in a small house near a fashionable square
Cared for by servants to the number of four.
Now when she died there was silence in heaven
And silence at her end of the street.
The shutters were drawn and the undertaker wiped his feet—
He was aware that this sort of thing had occurred before.
The dogs were handsomely provided for,
But shortly afterwards the parrot died too.
The Dresden clock continued ticking on the mantelpiece,
And the footman sat upon the dining-table
Holding the second housemaid on his knees—
Who had always been so careful while her mistress lived.

Starting with the well-bred name, as if on a visiting-card, the terms of the poem seem inviting us to scorn an existence so closed in. The 'maiden aunt', the 'fashionable' square, the facetiously aggrandized 'servants to the number of four'—and indeed the contrast between the genteel smallness of the house and the equally genteel-imposing size of the staff: all these touches tempt a condescending smile, as do the subsequent calamities of the parrot's demise, and the footman making play with the second housemaid. Even in their overthrow, Boston's refinements look absurd. Yet into the midst of this society's genteel life something has intruded after all: death, about which nothing can actually be said, though the undertaker is aware that 'this sort of thing had occurred before'. Socially, there are rituals to observe; the shutters are drawn, neighbours are respectfully quiet; but at the core of the poem both language and reader are left nonplussed at the event, like the young man in 'Portrait' wondering if he has the right to smile:

Now when she died there was silence in heaven
And silence at her end of the street.

It may be that death is mere extinction and all hopes of afterlife are vain; or it may be that the silence in heaven does indeed acknowledge death as a happening so momentous that the passage of the soul must be greeted as in Revelation 8: 1 when the seventh seal is opened and the end of all creation is ready to begin. Both possibilities present themselves, and there is no telling which to choose or how to interpret the two inscrutable lines; they remain the void into which we are brought to gaze.

To have opened this void in the midst of comedy makes 'Aunt Helen' a more significant poem than its conventional satirics first suggest. And just as significant again is the placing of it at the centre of *Prufrock and Other Observations*. Six poems precede and five follow this short piece, and it casts its own light or shadow over those nearby, so that turning back to 'The Boston Evening Transcript', for example, one sees with new intensity the suburban street like time itself down which the protagonist must labour. Once more, in the midst of mundane experience, a visionary gap appears. As it does in 'Mr Apollinax', whose faculty soirée disintegrates into the carnival of an 'irresponsible foetus', where a head might roll under a chair, Priapus loom in the shrubbery, and centaurs' hoofs beat the hard turf. By the time of 'Hysteria', even that (mock-classical) degree of coherence has been lost: the whole of experience is breaking up, till we can't be sure whose hysteria this is—his or hers—it seems so unlocateable amidst the fragmentation. But then we might notice that 'Hysteria' is itself an answer to other poems in the volume, especially 'Rhapsody on a Windy Night', with its beating street-lamps and crazed or abandoned women, and 'Conversation Galante', where the poeticizing ironist can see woman only as 'eternal humorist,/The eternal enemy of the absolute', so must experiment with one affectation then the next, to paper over the emptiness of human relations.

> I observe: 'Our sentimental friend the moon!
> Or possibly (fantastic, I confess)
> It may be Prester John's balloon
> Or an old battered lantern hung aloft. . . .'

The unreadable silence at the core of 'Aunt Helen' makes its own comment on these loquacities by which it is surrounded.

So, one poem answers another; a larger composition or symphonic arrangement begins to form: in short, Eliot's poems are not best read as if they were separate items from which a few favourites can be selected at random. That treatment might have done for a writer intent on 'self-expression', whose individual works could be regarded as leaves shaken loose by the creative spirit and falling higgledy-piggledy where they will. But with this *œuvre* we are given carefully put-together volumes which it makes sense to consider as a whole: in the case of the first volume, a composition extending all the way from 'The Love Song of J. Alfred Prufrock' to that other (transformed and transforming) love-song, 'La Figlia Che Piange', which concludes and leads out from the book.

The reader begins, therefore, with the gestures, the voices, the dissolving milieux of a world where passion exists only to be deflected and desire subdued. 'Let us go then, you and I', the opening poem invites us: into an evening which, though it might once have struck the wanderer as romantic and sublime—in Wordsworth's poetry, for instance ('It is a beauteous evening, calm and free')—now registers upon the senses no more than a parody of its lost celestial glory: the *ethereal* reduced numbingly to *ether*, 'Like a patient etherised upon a table'. Likewise the music of the piece, which, though it seeks the freedom of a love-song, keeps circling back to a timidly self-regarding refrain, '"Do I dare?" and "Do I dare?" . . . And would it have been worth it, after all . . . If one, settling a pillow by her head,/Should say: "That is not what I meant at all. That is not it at all"'. How can love be urged in verse like this, which turns to self-pitying elegy every chance it has?

More than the shortcomings of a private character, though, are brought into focus here. To read the Song as being about Prufrock's own failure of nerve is to reduce it all to 'personality' once again, whereas not only the detail of the writing but the shaping of the volume to which it lends its name has uncovered a larger condition, that of a society, a politics, a culture. When, in one long lyric swell, 'I grow old . . . I grow old' brings forth its own self-deflatingly heroic rhyme, and those rolled trousers then prepare the way for white flannel ones, and *peach* leads to *beach*, which in turn produces mermaids—

I have heard the mermaids singing, each to each

—we can measure this crest of yearning (and its immediate subsidence: 'I do not think that they will sing to me') against the other literatures it calls to mind. 'Teach me to heare Mermaides singing', wrote Donne in one of the confidently cynical love-songs the English Renaissance half-mocked-at and half-enjoyed. '*J'ai rêvé dans la grotte où nage la sirène*', sang Gérard de Nerval's disinherited prince ('El Desdichado') two-and-a-half centuries later, rhyming *his* mermaids with even more voluptuous dreams of sexual encounter: '*Mon front est rouge encor du baiser de la reine*'. 'I have dreamed in the grotto where the siren swims . . . my brow is still red with the kiss of the queen.' The sea-girls of 'Prufrock' never offer such passion as this; passion in fact is beyond the scope of the poem, for linger as it might in the chambers of the sea, that underwater world is plainly no substitute for the lamplit rooms, the solitudes and interrogations that elsewhere, up above, prove so formidable and yet alluring. The best the vision of sea-girls can offer is the knowledge of freedom that can never be attained—like the lost happiness the Forsaken Merman calls after in Matthew Arnold's poem (1849), as he feels 'the great winds shoreward blow' and must leave his mortal love behind. The final lines of 'Prufrock' gather up such moments as these out of the past of European culture, and from them produce not a new impetus towards life, so much as a plangent admission of defeat, as the consciousness which has invested itself in romantic dreams—'I have seen them riding seaward on the waves'—is summoned back to the surface of reality, and there fails: 'human voices wake us, and we drown'. A beautifully resonant last chord, but dismaying nonetheless.

Prufrock's failure, then (to draw the poem together for a moment under the heading of 'his' name), gives us a way of understanding the rest of the volume. If human voices, at the end of the Love-Song, kill by awakening to life, they speak more insistently than ever in 'Portrait of a Lady', the poem which, by a stroke of luck or brilliant calculation, Eliot placed straight after. The title carefully repeats that of the novel by Henry James, another American who sought his destiny in England; and James, bringing with him a whole refinement of civilization, is famous for extracting drama from every nuance of his characters' highly stylized speech. The insinuations of a rhythm, a sudden change of register, the drop into colloquialism or production of a cherished foreign term, these are cunningly exploited by the novelist and poet alike:

> 'You do not know how much they mean to me, my friends . . .
> How much it means that I say this to you—
> Without these friendships—life, what *cauchemar!*'

What is significant, though, is how quickly the civilized tones of the poem twist into a paranoia barely able to contain its feelings of rejection and unease:

> Among the windings of the violins
> And the ariettes
> Of cracked cornets
> Inside my brain a dull tom-tom begins
> Absurdly hammering a prelude of its own,
> Capricious monotone
> That is at least one definite 'false note.'

Something more than 'social comedy' is directing those ugly noises back against the woman, as though *she* were responsible for what is thumping and whining in the listener's head. Faced by her determination to remain herself—that over-fine self she has made—male discomfiture mounts to a kind of frenzy, in bear-dance, parrot cry and ape chatter, and then, in a final telling parabola, looks forward to the lady's death, as if that were the only way of dealing with her claims. For not even friendship, it now seems, is possible between men and women in the *Prufrock* world, let alone romantic friendship, let alone the various passions of love.

What *is* possible is, on the one side, a sort of desperation, and on the other, fascinated disgust. The sputtering street-lamp of 'Rhapsody on a Windy Night' directs your eyes to the woman hesitating towards you in a doorway which opens on her like a grin. It directs them again to a diseased harlot of a moon. Distasteful and yet inviting, femaleness pervades the poem, like smells which cross and cross across the brain, as dust and eau de cologne lead on to

> Smells of chestnuts in the streets,
> And female smells in shuttered rooms,
> And cigarettes in corridors
> And cocktail smells in bars.

Yet for us, if we take the whole shaped experience the poem has to offer, something more than revulsion is registered, all the same. The woman in the doorway, her dress torn and stained with sand, is as much a victim as a temptress; the moon is a deserted lunatic, pathetic and gruesomely coquettish; and meanwhile a world of poverty makes itself felt, with the starving cat and thieving child who pockets a toy on the quay. Consciousness may fasten on what disturbs and disgusts, but the poem reveals the consciousness in 'Rhapsody on a Windy Night' to be an alienated one, a memory shaken 'As a madman shakes a dead geranium'. It is like being possessed, where whispering lunar incantations undo the control of the mind, and the street-lamp issues its commands: *look here, look there, see horror*. To see the world in those terms is to give oneself no living space within it. Only skeletons remain. Not surprisingly, therefore, after the clock has told the dreadful night through to dawn, the lamp lights the way only to death. That is what 'life' comes to mean to a mind unable to forget its own appalled hallucinations, its revulsion and dismay.

The lamp said,
'Four o'clock.
Here is the number on the door.
Memory!
You have the key,
The little lamp spreads a ring on the stair.
Mount.
The bed is open; the tooth-brush hangs on the wall,
Put your shoes at the door, sleep, prepare for life.'

The last twist of the knife.

a gesture and a pose

A rhapsody may be exalted verse, lofty and eloquent as epic, or a poetry verging on madness. In the same way, the term might be used of music which is passionately improvisational, or music disconnected and incoherent. It signals a risk-taking art. Perhaps not surprisingly, therefore, in Eliot's first book of poems the 'Rhapsody on a Windy Night' is introduced by something seemingly more modest: four pieces identified as 'Preludes'.

They appear to be describing, summoning up, now this, now that, in a succession of glimpses of dingy rooms and city streets. But if description implies a describer, we will look in vain for such an entity here. The strategy of the verse is once again to make the scene *compose itself*, or seem to do so, as at the opening of 'Portrait of a Lady'; but this time with a yet more disconcerting animation. The winter evening settles down, as if with doggy companionableness.

At the opening of Prelude II, the morning likewise resumes a life of its own; it comes to consciousness without the aid of any human brain, and is conscious not of ideas but of sensations, 'faint stale smells of beer'. The night (in III) reveals the thousand sordid images of which your soul is constituted, and straightaway the old transcendent reality of Soul is replaced by flickering phantoms. Or the street tries but fails to understand your vision of it; or else (in IV) has a conscience 'Impatient to assume the world'. Everywhere the reader looks in 'Preludes' things are on the move—but in such a way as to cancel their observers out. For when a gusty shower wraps scraps of withered leaves about 'your' feet, the pronoun must be understood to refer to someone other than the you or me who reads. Someone, no one: you/not you, the poetry seems to say; and that is what it has been saying from the first line of the *Collected Poems* ('Let us go then, you and I') to its closing inscription of 'These . . . private words addressed to you in public'. Even when, in Prelude II,

> One thinks of all the hands
> That are raising dingy shades
> In a thousand furnished rooms

that thinking 'One' is undone straightaway, since syntax has already aligned it with 'the other masquerades/That time resumes', to make the pronoun signal not a self but a disguise or emptiness instead. The sentence contains no authoritative assertion of presence at all, only the transformation of one absence into another.

So object and subject, world and observer, disintegrate into a kind of music which is also a form of madness: an improvisation over the void. But the vision of the 'Rhapsody' and of the 'Preludes' is finally escaped from—and not through the flippancy of smart satiric exercises like energetic 'Cousin Nancy', but through the transforming intensity of lyric, in the last poem of the volume, 'La Figlia Che Piange'.

The first poem, 'Prufrock', had opened with lines from Dante; now, Dante's language returns to shape the closing title by calling to mind another *figlia che piange*, Francesca da Rimini, who will relate her tale, she says, as one who weeps and tells: '*dirò come colui che piange e dice*' (*Inferno* v. 126). Since the girl of Eliot's poem is not herself shown as weeping, Francesca's wraith has all the more presence, we may feel. But a Christian cosmology, and the pattern of judgement it embodies, is not the only one by which to understand what the poem offers. Straightaway this memory of a doomed and punished love is answered by a different voice again, this time producing words in Latin—'O *quam te memorem virgo*'—as if a still more ancient civilization spoke.[3] From Dante, we glance even further backwards to the *Aeneid* (I. 327), where Venus appeared to a son who could not recognize her or even know what she should be called. Only as she left him was her divinity revealed. And that may be the connection we need.

For what the poem centres upon is the vision of loss: only in parting can love be known for what it is. By parting, in fact, the girl's beauty is kept forever, 'Her hair over her arms and her arms full of flowers', whereas had she stayed with her lover, that moment of revelation would never have been; we should have lost 'a gesture and a pose'. It is a strange love that reveals itself through turning itself away, and which would rather lose the human presence in order to retain the image. But then, the *eros* of the poem is altogether strange, issuing commands to the girl which would render her into a succession of statuesquenesses, a silent aesthetic object:

Stand on the highest pavement of the stair—
Lean on a garden urn—
Weave, weave the sunlight in your hair—
Clasp your flowers to you with a pained surprise—
Fling them to the ground and turn
With a fugitive resentment in your eyes:
But weave, weave the sunlight in your hair.

Stranger still, however, is the resistance the vision itself offers to imagination as the imagination endeavours to perfect it. The girl does not (it seems) stand, lean, weave, turn, at the behest of the poem, for no sooner have we finished reading the first stanza, than the grammar of stanza two retrospectively recasts all those gestures.

So I would have had him leave,
So I would have had her stand and grieve,
So he would have left
As the soul leaves the body torn and bruised,
As the mind deserts the body it has used. . . .

'I would have had him leave', admits the poem, but that vision of a parting on male terms—he acting *soul* and *mind* to her idealized and passive *body*—happened only inside the momentary make-believe of art, and what art gives it can immediately take back again. 'So he would have left'—except that now, at this turn of the wording, he does not. Some other parting took place between them. And who is this 'he' in any case? Come to that, who is 'she'? By this last page of the *Prufrock* volume, the reader will be prepared for the elusiveness with which 'he' and 'I' half-resist, half-merge into one another, while the remaining pronoun is pure statement of the feminine, that which designates the Other. Author, reader, imagined actors: 'La Figlia Che Piange' is not a story so much as a happening in consciousness—*our* consciousness, aware that we are watching a poem being put together, yet no less strongly caught up in its states of mind and feeling. We are not invited to confuse verbal and actual worlds, as if the protagonists were real people; our task is precisely to observe that they are not. For just as the love the poem sings points beyond itself, away from natural attachment, so the poetry is made, not to sustain belief, but to be recognized as fiction, fabrication, a non-reality, yet one more potent than the living of ordinary life. Inside its order, human satisfactions are relinquished (having no place there, anyway) in order that perfections of a different sort may be achieved.

> She turned away, but with the autumn weather
> Compelled my imagination many days,
> Many days and many hours:
> Her hair over her arms and her arms full of flowers.
> And I wonder how they should have been together!
> I should have lost a gesture and a pose.
> Sometimes these cogitations still amaze
> The troubled midnight and the noon's repose.

It is an ending which prepares the way for the deepest moments of Eliot's later work. 'She turned away', and in doing so turned into a presence that lasts forever, 'Her hair over her arms and her arms full of flowers'. Desire and fascination which, through 'The Love Song of J. Alfred Prufrock', and 'Portrait', 'Rhapsody' and 'Hysteria', have troubled his poems so many different ways, are rewritten here into idealized gesture, with a renunciatory completeness quite enough to amaze whoever contemplates the poem.

2

REPLACINGS

Any writer who is widely read becomes, in time, as much the product of his own writings as they are of him. 'He' is a way of interpreting those texts which go under his name—so we construct the Emily Dickinson, Gertrude Stein or T. S. Eliot by means of which we read the printed poems. If the poems seem difficult, it may help to believe the author is very clever, and one belief in turn precipitates others. Around such crystals the stalagmite of legend will gradually accrete: the author is an intellectual, a holder of theories and beliefs, perhaps an élitist or separatist of some kind, consequently disdainful of ordinary readers, and quite possibly anti-democratic to boot. Rising up in this alarming way, Eliot the fascist has been a topic for concerned debate. The point is not that such legendary formations are wrong, but that they are culture-specific, and will alter therefore as their circumstances change. The fascist, the churchman, the neurotic, the student of philosophy, the unhappy husband, the elder statesman of literature: the various T. S. Eliots of the past seventy years cannot simply be ignored, lest they remain to exert an unadmitted pressure on our thought, and one of the fruitful achievements of recent years has been the seriousness with which the biography of this intensely private poet has been treated as a proper object of study.[4]

This is not to replace the poetry with the man who wrote it. On the contrary, Eliot now exists rather as Milton or Shakespeare does, as a literary experience, a body of written work. Yet the material onto which we project his name certainly came from somewhere. Like all writing, his belongs to its place and time—so to start at one beginning, we can remind ourselves that Thomas Stearns Eliot (his middle name is from his mother's family) was born in St Louis, Missouri, in September 1888. He was by some years the youngest of seven children, his parents respected and well-to-do in that city dominated by the presence of the great Mississippi, its steamboats, its commerce and its floods. In 1906, he entered Harvard, where over the next few years he encountered recent European literature and philosophy, and began to compose some of the earliest poems in *Prufrock*. After a year abroad, 1910–11, he returned to his American university and started work on a dissertation whose material would eventually be published as *Knowledge and Experience in the Philosophy of F. H. Bradley*. The onset of war in 1914 cut short his intended postgraduate studies in Germany, and he moved to England, where he remained in effect for the rest of his life. Married (1915), and settled in London, he published two books of poetry (1917 and 1920) and a collection of critical essays, *The Sacred Wood* (1920), before completing *The Waste Land*, which appeared in 1922. Long before his death in January 1965, he had become perhaps the most celebrated writer of his time.

Those facts represent one kind of understanding. Family and marital circumstances, educational success, publications—all these help us to fit a writer into the interlocking public systems of Western middle-class life. And in the process, they assume at the centre of the writing a continuous and solid entity: the Author. From this Author the poems flow, generated by Inspiration or some similarly mysterious thing. But it would be possible to represent the work of literature in quite a different fashion. Now, not author, but text might occupy the critic's full attention, on the grounds that a poem once written has detached itself from its writer. Instead of conveying to us a 'message' or some other form of authorial self-expression, it exists as a verbal event inside the field of language—subject, therefore, to the rules and conventions of the language, and the tactics and orientations which enable a reader to read. A more dramatic, if not melodramatic, way of putting that would undo the idea of authorship still further, and define the poet as simply the site on which the culture at this or that historical moment is *writing itself*, so that an author is not an originator of meaning, or even a person in any old-fashioned sense, but a phenomenon which, like everything else in its culture, *is being written by* the various discourses of the day. Capitalism, secularism, imperialism, biology, psychology, and innumerable other forces and factors, are responsible for producing both writer and written text—or so the account might go. Once again, this is neither a neutral nor a necessary view, but an ideological preference, designed to challenge those same institutions of Western middle-class belief the older view of authorship would support.

Follow the dance/Of the goldfinch at noon

Poetry may take a different course again. Theoretical perspectives of various kinds give us their own insights, but the abstract understanding is not the same as the imaginative-emotional-intellectual experience of encountering 'Gerontion', say. And although the processes which led to 'Gerontion' may sometimes be guessed at from their traces within the poem, all too often they lie irrecoverably far back. Still, Eliot has provided his own theoretical accounts of some of the forces producing his verse, and it may be worth noticing where his emphases fall. For a start, there is the insistence on place, the districts and landscapes of his youth.

A writer's art, he once said, 'must be based on the accumulated sensations of the first twenty-one years'.[5] 'Sensations' is the telling word in that proposition, and maybe the unexpected one. For a long time, attention was bent on the intellectuality of Eliot's verse, so that its sensuous presence had to be fitted in as an afterthought, so to speak. But his own stress habitually fell elsewhere. 'Only a part of an author's imagery,' he once declared, 'comes from his reading.'

> It comes from the whole of his sensitive life since early childhood. Why, for all of us, out of all that we have heard, seen, felt, in a lifetime, do certain images recur, charged with emotion, rather than others? The song of one bird, the leap of one fish, at a particular place and time, the scent of one flower, an old woman on a German mountain path, six ruffians seen through an open window playing cards at night at a small French railway junction where there was a water-mill: such memories may have symbolic value, but of what we cannot tell, for they represent

> the depths of feeling into which we cannot peer. We might just as well ask why, when we try to recall visually some period in the past, we find in our memory just the few meagre arbitrarily chosen set of snapshots that we do find there, the faded poor souvenirs of passionate moments.
>
> (*The Use of Poetry and the Use of Criticism*, p. 148)

In such a composition, 'place' is transformed into images, magnetized, as he said in the same set of lectures, by the poet's mind.

> There might be the experience of a child of ten, a small boy peering through sea-water in a rock-pool, and finding a sea-anemone for the first time: the simple experience (not so simple, for an exceptional child, as it looks) might lie dormant in his mind for twenty years, and re-appear transformed in some verse-context charged with great imaginative pressure.
>
> (pp. 78–9)

Of his own writing, he told an interviewer, 'in its sources, in its emotional springs, it comes from America',[6] and the various reminiscences he composed of his early years suggest how those emotional springs, from deep in his childhood in St Louis and on the Massachusetts coast, ran through and fertilized his poetry in sometimes unexpected ways.

> [T]here is something in having passed one's childhood beside the big river, which is incommunicable to those who have not. Of course my people were Northerners and New Englanders . . . but Missouri and the Mississippi have made a deeper impression on me than any other part of the world.

Or again:

> [My] family guarded jealously its connections with New England; but it was not until years of maturity that I perceived that I myself had always been a New Englander in the South West, and a South Westerner in New England . . . In New England I missed the long dark river, the ailanthus trees, the flaming cardinal birds, the high limestone bluffs where we searched for fossil shell-fish; in Missouri I missed the fir trees, the bay and goldenrod, the song-sparrows, the red granite and the blue sea of Massachusetts.

Any reader familiar with the *Collected Poems* will hear echoes backwards and forwards, catching up moments in *Ash Wednesday*, the 'Landscapes' of *c.* 1933–5, and *Four Quartets*. But the reader will notice, too, the continuing sense of displacement within the sense of place, absent features inside present ones, the absent seeming even more vivid perhaps—for to hear the song-sparrow is to miss the cardinal bird; to enjoy the ailanthus is to know that elsewhere, unforgettably, as witness *The Dry Salvages*, the fog is in the fir-trees. And some such sense, that in the midst of present life a greater reality is missing, comes through a number of the earliest poems Eliot chose to keep.[7] He may borrow his stage-properties and lyric forms from a nineteenth-century *ars melancholia*, but the intimations of mortality in these pre-Prufrock songs foreshadow the life's work still to come.

When we came home across the hill
  No leaves were fallen from the trees;
  The gentle fingers of the breeze
Had torn no quivering cobweb down.

The hedgerow bloomed with flowers still,
  No withered petals lay beneath;
  But the wild roses in your wreath
Were faded, and the leaves were brown.

('Song: When we came home across the hill')

In the midst of natural perfection a greater reality is missing—not because the here and now is thinly insufficient, but because of its very fullness of particularity, its own intactness. And the name of that which life (almost) obscures is Death, spoken however quietly by the browned leaves and faded roses. 'Song' was most likely written in May 1907; towards the end of the following year he wrote, in similarly old-fashioned yet clear-eyed stanzas, 'Before Morning'.

While all the East was weaving red with gray,
The flowers at the window turned toward dawn,
Petal on petal, waiting for the day,
Fresh flowers, withered flowers, flowers of dawn.

This morning's flowers and flowers of yesterday
Their fragrance drifts across the room at dawn,
Fragrance of bloom and fragrance of decay,
Fresh flowers, withered flowers, flowers of dawn.

'Fragrance of bloom and fragrance of decay' is not the idiom the older Eliot will employ, but death-in-life stays with him. To find death inside life becomes the aim, in fact; and then to be absolute for death. That last piece of advice is the Duke's injunction in *Measure for Measure* (III. i), and it provides the epigraph to 'Gerontion' a dozen years further on.

Still, only a dozen years. The development from *Poems written in Early Youth* was remarkably rapid and complete, even if one can see, looking back, much of the later writing already rehearsed in this small collection of juvenilia. By November 1909, Eliot could give a passable Englishing of the Romantic self-mockeries he had learnt from Jules Laforgue, whose verse he encountered at Harvard. So his own 'Nocturne', under the spell of Laforgue, rewrites the passion of *Romeo and Juliet* into 'The usual debate/Of love, beneath a bored but courteous moon. . . . in my best mode oblique', and the fastidious cynicisms of the style become a weapon to use in prising open the emptiness of 'life'. 'Humoresque' ('One of my marionettes is dead') is even more surgical, in dispatching the poem's poor creature of fashion to Limbo, yet allowing him his spectral pathos all the same, while 'Spleen' (1910) and 'The Death of Saint Narcissus' (1915) carry us still further away from any satisfaction in the common ordinary world.

Come under the shadow of this gray rock

Prufrock and Other Observations appeared in June 1917 but most of the poems in it had been written some years before. By 1917, indeed, a number had made their way into print via periodicals in England and America, and Eliot's fear was that he had already written all the poetry he had it in him to write. 'Any poet, if he is to survive as a writer beyond his twenty-fifth year, must alter', he declared (*Selected Essays*, p. 15), having turned thirty a while before; and self-alteration certainly is one of the striking features of the work he now produced.

Some of it is not even written in the same language. In a

determination to embrace new influences, new possibilities, there were poems composed in French: 'Le Directeur', 'Lune de Miel', 'Dans le Restaurant', etc., *c.*1916–17. Other pieces modelled themselves on continental writers at one remove, or on Jacobean verse-drama, chronologically and rhetorically more remote. The various efforts eventually printed as *Poems 1920* are more brilliant, violent and puzzling than anything in the *Prufrock* collection. Demanding though they are, however, some of their bewildering shifts of angle come into focus when we see them as performances—drama in masks. Such presentations simultaneously conceal and betray the actor, just as Eliot's prose writings of the same period prescribe 'impersonality' for the artist, and at the same time make a highly individualistic show of their own advice. 'Poetry is not a turning loose of emotion, but an escape from emotion; it is not the expression of personality, but an escape from personality', declares 'Tradition and the Individual Talent'—going on to add, 'But, of course, only those who have personality and emotions know what it means to want to escape from these things'. These are stirring claims, not least in their calculated affront to the ordinary reader's ordinary self-knowledge. What we might have thought of as 'our' emotions are scorned as having no existence at all. Which makes it as cool a piece of self-assertion on the writer's part as one could fear to find.

So the theoretical proposals of 1919—

> The progress of an artist is a continual self-sacrifice, a continual extinction of personality
>
> ('Tradition and the Individual Talent')

> *Qua* work of art, the work of art cannot be interpreted; there is nothing to interpret; we can only criticize it according to standards
>
> ('Hamlet')

> The creation of a work of art, we will say the creation of a character in a drama, consists in the process of transfusion of the personality, or, in a deeper sense, the life, of the author into the character. This is a very different matter from the orthodox creation in one's own image
>
> ('Ben Jonson': all reprinted in *Selected Essays*)

—stand alongside the poetry, not as explanations of it, so much as other strategies of command, other ways of 'extinguishing' personality, by monumentalizing it into doctrine, or transfusing the author's 'life' into particular formations of words. The essays are powerful impositions on the reader, partly because their demand is not to be critically interrogated ('there is nothing to interpret'), only to be confronted and taken in. And what, above all, they want taken in is the declared absence of the self. The poet's mind is to be a receptacle, or a tantalus jar, or a shred of platinum, inert and neutral in itself until the proper conditions obtain; it is a place where 'impressions and experiences combine in peculiar and unexpected ways'.

> The more perfect the artist, the more completely separate in him will be the man who suffers and the mind which creates.
>
> ('Tradition and the Individual Talent', *Selected Essays*, pp. 17 ff.)

For Eliot, though, as it happened, poetry, criticism, and remembered experience came together with unforeseen intensity in the summer of 1919, to make possible a new movement in his career. Asked to review an autobiography, *The Education of Henry Adams*, by a fellow New Englander, he found depicted there a man who, caught between aspiration and doubt, could commit himself to nothing; 'wherever he stepped, the ground did not simply give way, it flew into particles' ('A Sceptical Patrician', *Athenaeum*, 23 May 1919). Fractured atoms, an unreality felt within reality itself—there are various attitudes possible to this, but Adams's predicament was the Boston predicament, felt Eliot, one he himself had not wholly escaped; a failure of spiritual rigour, a disablement of belief. Yet, like Adams, he had known very different Americas too: St Louis, as against genteel Boston; ailanthus and goldenrod, river and sea, as against the refinements of cultivation. And during these weeks in London, in a different springtime again, as April led on towards June, the autobiography re-evoked for him those other experiences, challenging in their pagan power: 'dogwood and judas-tree . . . the brooding heat of the profligate vegetation . . . terrific splendour of the June thundergust . . . intermixture of delicate grace and passionate depravity that marked the Maryland May'. Visions of this kind, 'sensual, animal, elemental', which Adams would repudiate but know no deeper way of understanding, released in Eliot 'accumulated sensations of [his own] first twenty-one years', now brought to book in a formidably alien context: 'Gerontion'. It was a means of starting to remake the literary self.

One clue is what happened to the words absorbed from *The Education of Henry Adams*. Like all the matter grafted into the poem, from scripture, drama, and so on, the American phrasings are made to flourish on new stock—disturbingly, alarmingly, new.

In the juvescence of the year
Came Christ the tiger

In depraved May, dogwood and chestnut, flowering judas,
To be eaten, to be divided, to be drunk
Among whispers; by Mr. Silvero
With caressing hands. . . .

Adams's dogwood and judas-tree had merely descriptive value as items in the landscape, whereas 'flowering judas' in this new ensemble casts a sinisterly luxuriant shade. But not because the perspective in which it takes its place is a Christian one. On the contrary, what has entered the poem with 'Christ the tiger' is something uncapturable. The three words leap into emptiness; they are given, and for a moment, nothing happens—only a wordless blank, a silence that can neither be interpreted nor ignored; after which, the verse resumes. Yet on the further side of that silence, everything has changed. For 'Christ the tiger' is indeed definitive, but not as orthodoxy might expect. Instead, on the announcement of that arrival, juvescence turns to corruption—not even natural fertility, but a maytime actually 'depraved'; and then, as the syntax further uncoils, the energy of the apparition is transformed, the active made passive, its former terror now an unspoken something to be eaten, divided, drunk—sacramentally, one might say, if it were not that the signs of grace, everywhere at hand, are everywhere darkened and diverted. What divinity is it that a Mr. Silvero will caress?

Signs are taken for wonders. 'We would see a sign!'
The word within a word, unable to speak a word,
Swaddled with darkness.

It was an evil and adulterous generation (Matt. 12: 39) that cried

'We would see a sign!', and the cry is answered now, in this fearsomely *dis*comforting poem, where signs are given alright, but what they signify who can say, when 'word within a word, unable to speak a word' leaves us unable to decide if such significations tell anything at all. Once, perhaps, they did. When Archbishop Lancelot Andrewes wrote his Christmas sermon of 1618, it was the Logos of which he spoke, '*Verbum infans*, the Word without a word; the eternal Word not able to speak a word'. Three hundred years later, however, 'Gerontion' can produce no Word, no Godhead, only words which baffle us with their self-repeating as they echo back and forth. Worse still, the lines declare their own language never *can* show what it has to say, being 'swaddled'—as at Bethlehem maybe, but just as plausibly by mere incapacity, a darkness in which there is nothing to see and any recollection of the gospel is only another mistake.

So the poetry proceeds, unwriting itself in accumulations of echo, allusion, and utterance where every new move dislodges what has gone before. We have not reached the conclusion even when 'The tiger springs in the new year. Us he devours', since that in turn precipitates a 'Think at last', which is no 'last' but only the first of a sequence of further lines. To be eaten by Christ, appalling though the thought may be, is no possible climax or stop to the poem, only one more of the momentous imaginings which weave and reweave the wind on vacant shuttles, as knowledge unfolds itself into futility, apocalyptic terrors rear up and disappear, and the ending leaves the tenants of the house still whispering like inexorcizable ghosts.

It used to be standard to describe 'Gerontion' as a dramatic monologue, as if what comprised the poem were the thoughts of 'a dry brain in a dry season', a withered Polonius, say.[8] And ingenuity still labours to fashion a setting where these looked-for ruminations can take place:

> The house in which Gerontion lives, clearly on the edge of doom, is old, decayed, brittle, windowless, draughty; it is located in a neglected yard composed of rocks, moss, excreta. The tenants—Gerontion and a woman—are old and sick. . . .
>
> (Jewel Spears Brooker, 'Substitutes for Christianity in the Poetry of T. S. Eliot', in Olney [1988], p. 50)

and so on, usually rising to remarks about the owner and the possible location of goat-pastures ('overhead'). But this makes everything banal. The first words of the text position its action in *us*.

Like 'Prufrock', it begins with its epigraph. 'Thou hast nor youth nor age', declares the great writer here appropriated: Shakespeare, hailed by the English as not of an age but for all time. *You, reader*, his words say to us, since who else is left to be addressed by them, now that a later poet has lifted them out of the function they once had in *Measure for Measure* (rewriting them as well, so that Shakespeare's 'dreaming on both' becomes our century's 'dreaming *of*')? But even before the epigraph entangles us in its pronoun, our educated understanding has already been called on by the title. A 'transliteration of the Greek word for little old man', according to Southam's *Student's Guide*, it is more importantly a reminiscence of the once-famous *Dream of Gerontius*, a series of verse-tableaux by Cardinal Newman. The twentieth century had been ushered in by Elgar's setting of these poems; in 1900 it seemed possible, for that composer anyway, to depict the Old Age of Victorian hope as making its way towards salvation. But 1919 does not contemplate such pilgrimage; the very word the poem takes to name itself confesses how shrunken life is from that noble dream. Now, what is seen as nature's end is not 'the Holiest in the Height',[9] but mere obliteration—'White feathers in the snow, the Gulf claims'—and this Gerontion is no spiritual entity, like Newman's penitential Old Man. It is not even a person, but a signifier, a verbal function: the point through which we enter an activity of consciousness. Our consciousness, necessarily, for the time we stay, making 'I' the place where *we* are in the poem, reading.

So, 'Here I am . . .': inside a poem, that is. And immediately its action starts to complicate and close around us. For the text speaks with many voices, some of which we can hardly help hearing after decades of commentary and exposition.

> Here I am, an old man in a dry month . . .

However 'symbolic' that old man may feel to be (the spiritual aridity of a dying world, etc.), the opening words are not Eliot's alone, but another quotation—this time from a biography of Edward Fitzgerald, Victorian translator of the *Rubáiyát of Omar*

Khayyám: a vanished ethos celebrating vanished passions.[10] And then again, 'old man' may echo that other old man, the Adam or body of sin, which in Romans 6: 6 Paul calls to be crucified with Christ. Meanwhile, the 'hot gates' of the next sentence translate—without naming—Thermopylae, while the 'salt marsh', the 'cutlass', summon other wars and subjugations and buccaneering feats. A panorama of heroisms, sensual, secular, spiritual, has unfolded within a few lines. For Gerontion, though, the great choices were negated even before they came into view; he was neither there, nor there, nor there . . . which is to say, more literally following the poem, 'I' was not—and with that realization, the grammar twists us back into the present tense, to focus on that 'I' and interrogate what it is.

It is the 'I' of a particular moment in history that places itself in the 'decayed house' of the following lines. To this point, the language of the poem has been rather noticeably plain; no one at least would stumble over diction until 'some estaminet' is reached—but at that word, the reader hesitates, perhaps. Because 'estaminet' is markedly foreign. It was imported into English during the early 1800s, and Thackeray flourished it knowingly in *Vanity Fair* (1848); but in Eliot's poem (1919) it speaks its new historical moment precisely, as a specimen of the argot brought back from France by the troops of the 1914–18 war. *Estaminet: a cafe in which smoking is allowed*: around this border-crossing word twentieth-century experience congregated, already loaded with a sense of dirt and danger.

> My house is a decayed house,
> And the jew squats on the windowsill, the owner,
> Spawned in some estaminet of Antwerp,
> Blistered in Brussels, patched and peeled in London.

So the text stood until 1963, when a misguided caution prompted its author to raise 'jew' to a capital letter. Yet that attempt to respectabilize the line in effect only makes it worse. The original phrasing does not pretend to be anything but abuse, whereas, revised, it looks as if it actually does mean Jews. But the point is surely that language, whatever a writer's intentions, declares where it has been, shows the minds that have kept it company; and in this passage what we see is language revelling in base disgusts. So 'Jew', it makes us realize, *has* been a horror-word, a term of execration. Contemptuously lowered further yet, decapitalized, it is an adjective or verb of damage. To *jew down* = to beat down and cheat (1825); to *outjew* = to outdo a usurer; *jewboy*; *jewbail*, insults both of them; *jew-slime* (= asphalt, bitumen, mortar, with the authority behind it of Genesis 11: 3): the dictionaries trace the history through which that lower-case *jew* has reached us, and under such a history even place-names (Antwerp, Brussels, London) become the sign not so much of homeless dispossession as of the un-get-riddable pervasiveness of the Semite. The long shamefulness of our own time's treatment of the Jews is written into the lines—and that it is precisely 'our' time is what makes the experience so disturbing.

> The Jew 'squats' (an undoubted filament to 'merds' here), is 'spawned', 'blistered', 'patched' and 'peeled' in a swift aggressive flurry of strong verbs. One can scarcely avoid an impression of inflicted retaliations. Here is the 'jew' placarded, as owner, on an appositional sill, being spattered, degraded and mutilated. Like a veritable Elder of Zion he is made to exemplify the squalor he is accused of causing. Yet the attack is at the same time deftly distanced. The indefiniteness of 'some' is furthered by the allusive knowingness of 'estaminet'. The reader finds himself divided between levels of aggression and disdain which may turn out to be an attack on him.
>
> (Gabriel Pearson, 'Eliot: an American use of symbolism', in Martin [1970], p. 87)

Do we collude in those inflicted retaliations, those presentations of 'the jew' as something simian and befouling, or do we hold aloof? Either way, whether we associate or dissociate ourselves, the strategy will blame us; and since that point is not grasped often enough, I want to argue that it is central. 'Gerontion' is not a poem about a character, any more than it is about the author himself. It is a text which implicates its reader in the act of reading it. Things would be easier if we *could* shift responsibility onto some persona and attribute all our discomfitures to him, but the mind is not permitted such safe disdain. Through Gerontion, we, being reader and speaker both at once, confront ourselves, as in a hall of mirrors, 'you' and 'I', reflexive pronouns enabling the operations of the poem to go on.

So, through cunning passages which reveal themselves as textual (passages of quotation/verse-pastiche) and, simultaneously, sexual (metaphors for the passages of the body), we are lured to think our way: down contrived corridors, 'And issues'—there, a momentary mock-release—into whispering ambitions, vanities, supple confusions. History is no more trustworthy than the common favours of a whore, 'giving' to anyone whose needs will pay her. But no one is invited to condemn. On the contrary, all alike are caught in unnatural vices and impudent crimes; and the climax comes when the mortal weaknesses we all share turn at last into universal pain:

> These tears are shaken from the wrath-bearing tree.

It is a fearsome vision.

Alongside 'Gerontion', how protected the experience of that matching monologue of old age (pre-Christian history's Old Age), 'Journey of the Magi', feels. 'A cold coming we had of it', declares the voice of the Magus, remembering being led to the end of the world, not for some revelation of glory, but only for a birth that was 'bitter agony . . . like Death'. Nevertheless, confronted though he is by a mystery that would dislocate every category of reassurance, he is not moved to participate in the pain and need—or even the ordinary experience—of his world. He remains, as he always was, the privileged outsider. To him, the camel men 'wanting their liquor and women' are hardly closer or more comprehensible than the camels. It is the same with the places through which he passes: all are alien, 'hostile . . . unfriendly . . . dirty'. And even the temperate valley at dawn, 'Wet, below the snow line, smelling of vegetation', has its life fixed portentously in his mind, as a series of actions whose meanings—whose actors, even—are absent, people having been replaced by mere bodily operations:

> Six hands at an open door dicing for pieces of silver,
> And feet kicking the empty wine-skins.

The reader can identify significances (Judas's pieces of silver, for example) the Magus cannot see. Always, that is the pattern; but it makes 'Journey of the Magi' a rather small-minded poem: a poem about the inadequate consciousness, the consciousness superior to its world—so it retreats into tepid semi-feelings ('we regretted . . . we preferred . . . it was (you may say) satisfactory')—but it could never have uncovered the reality of the Incarnation anyway. The Magus will never know what those empty wine-skins, or dicing hands, or three trees on the low sky, stand for. Only the new dispensation will reveal their place in the story, whereas the old men simply came too soon.

Unaware of Christ the Tiger, therefore, the Magi return to their places, 'these Kingdoms', where all they can do is wait for another death. The logic of 'Gerontion' is thus completed, from the other side (1927) of Eliot's conversion to Christianity, but the result is a poem far less intense, less alarming; in the end, less seriously religious.

For one thing, 'Gerontion' has the disruptive energy of wit. Even as the shocks and jars of the writing are registered, its exuberance makes itself felt. Take the comedy (more than comedy) of the names, Mr. Silvero, Madame de Tornquist, Mrs. Cammel. Or take the verve with which a sleepy figure of speech may be suddenly roused to life—as when the lines turn round on themselves asking, 'What will the spider do,/Suspend its operations?'. Nothing surer, of course; cobwebs will be hung up. And the dark joke is that for a spider to suspend its work in *this* way does not so much divert as precisely reinforce its power, just as to translate unmentionables into stylish Gallicism ('merds') heightens, by suppressing, impropriety. The text is a tissue of such linguistic repositionings, taking the ground away from under plodding feet.

The whole imaginary effect is too startling a contrivance to be laid at the door of any such persona (old man, dry brain, dull head among windy spaces) as the commentators describe. We can let that stable identity of the monologist go. But it is certainly true that presences, caricatures, puppet-figures if not personae, dominate *Poems 1920*, from Gerontion to Grishkin to Sweeney. The pattern is set at the start. And the collection's opening movement likewise draws the analytic arc most of the quatrain poems will follow—

> Rocks, moss, stonecrop, iron, merds —

where life heaves upwards, from mineral, through organism, only to be inexorably reclaimed. In silhouette, that is what the subsequent pieces outline, as their verses capture Apeneck Sweeney, or Grishkin's feline smell, or the lustreless protrusive eye staring from protozoic slime at a Venice of remnants in 'Burbank with a

Baedeker'. ('Pathos, piety, courage', murmurs the echo in the Marabar Caves; 'they exist, but are identical, and so is filth': E. M. Forster, *A Passage to India*, 1924, ch. xiv.) Such reductionism is a constant possibility for intelligence, and post-war Modernism found it simultaneously shocking and tempting: witness the grotesqueries which dominate *Poems 1920*—the daffodil bulbs instead of eyeballs, the oval O cropped out with teeth, or the horror-burlesque of an epileptic fit in a brothel: 'Gesture of orang-outang/Rises from the sheets in steam'.

Only the Hippopotamus, reclining broad-backed in the middle of the book, provides the comic counterpoint to Sweeney Erect. Now, creation is seen not as evolving towards its return to earth again, but quite the contrary: rising triumphant out of mud to be borne, redeemed, into heaven.

This latter-day Epistle to Laodiceans is the most plainly satirical of the poems, yet nimbler, more elusive than its central figure might suggest. The hippopotamus on his belly could hardly be more down to earth; but what does solidity rest on? Is it really real? The phrasing insinuates a doubt.

> Although he seems so firm to us
> He is merely flesh and blood.

The mind is to look, therefore, beyond these mere substantials.

> Flesh and blood is weak and frail,
> Susceptible to nervous shock;
> While the True Church can never fail
> For it is based upon a rock.

The frailty of hippos, all nerves, is not what we expected to have to consider. It is surely simple prejudice, however, that would deny the hippopotamus his sensibility, and pigheaded blindness that would claim flesh and blood *aren't* weak? Since they are so mortal, therefore, the Church is surely right to base itself on something higher? Except that, higher turns out to be lower, if we compare a rock with a living creature. At this point, therefore, the lines invite us to read them with different eyes. For the 'rock' on which the Church is based is Peter, or more exactly (according to Matthew 16: 18) it is faith, the faith which discerns that Christ is truly present, and the Messiah is come. Lower now becomes higher after all, by grounding itself on metaphor—acts of imaginative faith—rather than statements of the here and now. For however reliable the latter may appear, the material realm turns out to be one of uncertainty and fruitless striving. 'The 'potamus can never reach/ The mango on the mango-tree', whereas the True Church is shown as nourished and enriched beyond all human power. It can sleep and feed as effectively as watch and pray, since it feeds and rests upon God. Indeed, God having already redeemed (that is, bought back) His faithful, the Church need never stir 'to gather in its dividends'—and the comic surprise of the phrasing reminds us that *both* figures of speech are financial.

Such comedy works by remobilizing theological metaphors, thus causing them to be thought through again. 'Higher' is not *identified* with 'lower'—salvation with cash, hippo's mating call with the ecstasy of the mystics—but (quite the contrary) distinguished by being placed side by side, as parallels whose precision of limning ensures they cannot meet. By the time the 'potamus takes wing and enters heaven, the joke is not that so many tonnes of flesh and blood have been enskied and sainted, but rather that the hippo's bulk, while still kept sight of, has had to be utterly changed: it must take to the harp; must be embraced and kissed, washed white as snow. And so, against nature, it is. The material creation enters paradise by being (comically) transformed, while the True Church remains below, 'Wrapt in the old miasmal mist'—which may be a sign of its corruption, but just as plausibly a sign of *ours*, lost in a spiritual fog which prevents our ever seeing that the Christ of faith, though hidden from unbelievers' eyes, is eternally in our midst. The joke is on those who failed to take the wit of this satire seriously enough.

The smoky candle-end of time/Declines

'The Hippopotamus' would be the funniest poem Eliot wrote (it leaves the Practical Cats for dead), but it is a sensible choice to draw together the pattern of the 'Gerontion' book. Here, around an unreachable vision concealed by miasmal mist, the rest of the poems are clustered. Which means that either side of 'The Hippopotamus' are enigmatic pieces in French; further out from the centre come 'Burbank with a Baedeker' and 'Whispers of Immortality', mocking the unrealities of 'culture' and 'passion' together;

while 'Mr. Eliot's Sunday Morning Service', a semi-climax to *Poems 1920*, exposes 'religion' to the withering gaze of minds that can make nothing of it.

There are a lot of inverted commas in the preceding sentence. There is a lot of sceptical verve in this phase of Eliot's writing. If it allows the long-dead painter his vision of the Baptized God—as in the 'Sunday Morning Service':

> But through the water pale and thin
> Still shine the unoffending feet

—it returns obsessively to its task of presenting human creatures as animals, automata, articulated strings of bone and prejudice moving against a backcloth of grandeurs they hardly know. Bleistein could never identify the allusions, the quotations from Gautier, Shakespeare, Browning, Henry James, which define his situation for us, any more than the Cooking Egg could explain his relation to Rossetti's Blessed Damozel ('We two shall lie together, lapt/In a five per cent. Exchequer Bond').[11] The volume concludes with one of the most tantalizing of poems, 'Sweeney Among the Nightingales'—the title not only a reminiscence of Elizabeth Barrett Browning's 'Bianca Among the Nightingales' (1862), but recalling its own historical moment too: September 1918, when men in brown, the horrors of war still close at hand, might go in search of ladies of the night, whores, or, as the slang term more delicately called them, 'nightingales'.

It is a surreal encounter, this coming together of low and high. Apeneck Sweeney coexists with King Agamemnon, slaughtered again at the end and opening the poem with his dying words as epigraph. Drunken antics are performed by savagely X-rayed figures, like the silent vertebrate in brown, or Rachel with her murderous paws, or the man in the doorway reduced to a golden grin of his flashily filled teeth—and all these are set within a music of omen and dream and sacred tragedy.

> The circles of the stormy moon
> Slide westward toward the River Plate,
> Death and the Raven drift above
> And Sweeney guards the hornéd gate.
>
> Gloomy Orion and the Dog
> Are veiled; and hushed the shrunken seas;

The person in the Spanish cape
Tries to sit on Sweeney's knees

Slips and pulls the table-cloth
Overturns a coffee-cup,
Reorganised upon the floor
She yawns and draws a stocking up . . .

Not until the closing lines, however, does the music rise over the poem's pictured violence and disorder to carry them into a new world of feeling; but that is what it finally (astonishingly) does. The Great War of 1914–18, the Trojan War from which Agamemnon returned only to be slain by his wife, the frowzy dive where Sweeney looks for his good time, the wood within which Oedipus went to his death and was greeted by the gods: these are brought together in the climax, as if all times are one time and life is a transience, a brief moment of wrongdoing we can be satisfied to leave behind.

The host with someone indistinct
Converses at the door apart,
The nightingales are singing near
The Convent of the Sacred Heart,

And sang within the bloody wood
When Agamemnon cried aloud
And let their liquid siftings fall
To stain the stiff dishonoured shroud.

It is a wonderful end to the volume, matching Gerontion's obliteration with death of a different kind, in which the nightingales of Oedipus' release coexist with a reminder of Christ's willingness to die. In the midst of tawdriness, even horror, a larger pattern is discerned; the Sacred Heart, be-nunned and conventualized, yet still an emblem of suffering love, is juxtaposed with the sacred grove at Colonus where nightingales sing as Oedipus is given 'a passing more wonderful than that of any other man'. Nonetheless, there is no warming glow of optimism here. The last word of the post-war, preconversion *Poems* is, quite fittingly, 'shroud'.

3

In Different Voices

At the end of that strange, pained poem 'Dans le Restaurant', after the dilapidated waiter has told his frightening-pathetic tale, after the soup-eater has registered disgust and shame and a sort of horrified sympathy at the old man still gnawed by a longing for rapture—after all this, a voice strikes up from some depth no other piece in *Poems 1920* touched:

> Phlébas, le Phénicien, pendant quinze jours noyé,
> Oubliait les cris des mouettes et la houle de Cornouaille,
> Et les profits et les pertes, et la cargaison d'étain:
> Un courant de sous-mer l'emporta très loin,
> Le repassant aux étapes de sa vie antérieure.

Famous lines, of course, or almost famous, since the version we most likely know (from *The Waste Land*, IV) is only approximate to this, and anyway in English, not in French. But the surge and sweep of music here is, if anything, even stronger: 'les cris des mouettes et la houle de Cornouaille,/Et les profits et les pertes'. Only as Phlebas vanishes into the whirlpool does 'Death by Water' surpass its predecessor, and even then the relation between the two poems remains to puzzle the mind. It is not only that they share the vision of a life being repossessed by nature, but that this moment pivotal to *The Waste Land* was not originally composed for that poem at all.

Rather, we might almost claim the 1922 poem was composed for the sake of already-existent episodes like this. That would be to exaggerate, no doubt—and yet it underlines the extraordinary potency such pieces had for their author. At one point after another, the drafts of *The Waste Land* show what he meant when he recalled his experience as a maker of verse:

> I know that a poem, or a passage of a poem, may tend to realize itself first as a particular rhythm before it reaches expression in words, and that this rhythm may bring to birth the idea and the image . . .
>
> ('The Music of Poetry', p. 38)

Not the idea, or even the image at first, but deeper than either, the rhythm: 'A woman drew her long black hair out tight/And fiddled whisper music on those strings': lines which now seem integral to 'What the Thunder Said' (v. 377–84) were composed years earlier, probably by 1914, if not before; and amongst all the rephrasings they went through, it is their music that persists. Similarly with 'After the torchlight red on sweaty faces' (v. 322–30), or the episode which Eliot intended to publish as a single poem, 'The Death of Saint Narcissus', in 1915, only to give it its resting-place at last, unforgettably, in 'The Burial of the Dead' (I. 25–30):

> (Come in under the shadow of this red rock),
> And I will show you something different from either
> Your shadow at morning striding behind you
> Or your shadow at evening rising to meet you

In all such cases, '[t]he poem comes before the form, in the sense that the form grows out of the attempt of somebody to say something',[12] and the form of *The Waste Land* revealed itself gradually, over years. It was not at all clear, for instance, just what was to be included—so, even as late as January 1922 there was still a chance that 'Gerontion' would be part of the final work. It was Ezra Pound, friend and fellow American poet, *il miglior fabbro*, who got that distraction out of the way. And the practical criticism Pound bestowed on the mass of materials Eliot brought him has been justly praised, but sometimes as if what he did was to help

Eliot to solder discrete fragments together so as to make them a single thing—whereas, I don't think Eliot tried to achieve such unity. He changed, recombined, rearranged the *Waste Land* materials with phenomenal humility and open-mindedness, as his own self-criticism urged him, and as prompted by Pound. But although the result was ultimately a work which Pound could boast 'now runs from "April . . ." to "shantih" without a break. That is 19 pages, and let us say the longest poem in the English langwidge',[13] it remained strikingly discontinuous, the gaps, the change of voices being part of its imaginative action. Links of thought, or an ordered narrative sequence, never were part of the poem Eliot conceived. As he once remarked, self-deprecatingly, it always had been structureless, 'only in a more futile way' than the *Waste Land* which finally appeared.[14]

Over the seventy years since then, the poem has formed its readers. If it is more approachable now than it was in 1922, that is partly because a lot of hindrances (false expectations, and the like) have fallen away, and partly also because it is no longer an isolated phenomenon—though actually, even in 1922, the reader who had followed Eliot's work through the two preceding volumes was already in a good position to begin to hear the piece. For each of those volumes has a pattern somewhat as this poem does. Or perhaps one should rather talk of 'patterns', since there is no single structure to be unearthed, but instead a variety of ways in which the separate pieces of *Prufrock* or *Poems 1920* can be understood to relate to one another. Some of their interrelations we have already seen: the placing of 'La Figlia Che Piange' to answer the opening 'Love-Song of J. Alfred Prufrock'; the silence at the centre of 'Aunt Helen' which is itself at the centre of the book; the Hippopotamus rising skywards from the middle of a frieze of Sweeneys. All these are ways of organizing the individual items so that they radiate significances amongst themselves.

Similarly with the shaping of *The Waste Land*, which eventually resulted in a poem in five movements. This shape, which Eliot was to use again in each of the four *Quartets*, delays and displaces the centre so that it comes now not at the middle of the opus, but later, deeper in—requiring the reader to reach further.

IV. Death by Water

Phlebas the Phoenician, a fortnight dead,

Forgot the cry of gulls, and the deep sea swell
And the profit and loss.
                                        A current under sea
Picked his bones in whispers. As he rose and fell
He passed the stages of his age and youth
Entering the whirlpool.
                                        Gentile or Jew
O you who turn the wheel and look to windward,
Consider Phlebas, who was once handsome and tall as you.

It might have been an occasion of horror or jeering disgust; the drafts of *The Waste Land* show that such feelings weren't far below the surface.[15] But the lyric the poem finally achieved is eerily pure and cool. Sounds grow distant, fears and distractions no longer trouble the mind; the rise and fall of the drowned body is like the deep breathing of sleep; yet this is death, not life, and the grave movement of the lines does not shirk the knowledge of the corpse decomposing through the stages of age and youth. Picked clean, Phlebas enters the whirlpool and is taken from sight, while up above are those still in the world who turn the wheel and look to windward, as though to start again; not forgetting death, but not in thrall to it either. The vanished life is over, and calmly accepted, contemplated, as being so.

It is very different from the corpse which threatened to sprout, bloom, break from its bed at the end of 'The Burial of the Dead'. It is different, too, from desert nightmares, where death might be longed for but all that is given is 'fear in a handful of dust'. Throughout the poem to this point the only rest the spirit knows is through exhaustion or defeat, so that whatever moment of release may come, an annulling lethargy follows; but in 'Death by Water' dissolution itself takes on an active, renewing power. Such a death becomes the goal of the poem's life.

Shall these bones live? shall these/Bones live?

It is easy enough to see what the mind might wish to escape from in the desert sequences, or the 'crowds of people, walking round in a ring' evoked by Madame Sosostris, or the hallucinatory London inhabited by 'mon semblable,—mon frère!'. But the poem opens with a reversal of hope more startling than any of these. Spring time, which renews the dead land, brings no promise of renewal to the consciousness forming itself here:

> April is the cruellest month, breeding
> Lilacs out of the dead land, mixing
> Memory and desire, stirring
> Dull roots with spring rain.

Even the present participles, 'breeding . . . mixing . . . stirring', do not so much carry thought onwards as drag it, heavy and unwilling, over the end of each line. To retreat into deadness—'Winter kept us warm'—becomes, in this climate of feeling, a relief. And the further back we go, the easier it seems: to retreat from the pain of fertility, to comfort and forgetfulness, and then to a time ('Summer surprised us') recalled from a vanished world. Someone's world, but whose is it, this Munich of public parks and resorts, this moment not even of happiness especially but just of things done, voices heard, unattached to people, anonymous:

> we stopped in the colonnade,
> And went on in sunlight, into the Hofgarten,
> And drank coffee, and talked for an hour.
> Bin gar keine Russin, stamm' aus Litauen, echt deutsch

—where speakers and situations are equally unknown. One cannot say what animosity, pride or panic might lie behind the foreign words ('I'm not a bit Russian, come from Lithuania, a real German'); foreign they remain. But being so, they are safely distant; whatever hints of the breakup of Europe we read into them, such passionless memories can harm no one. Even the voice that now recalls from childhood a moment of fear and delight—

> He said, Marie,
> Marie, hold on tight. And down we went.
> In the mountains, there you feel free

—no sooner summons that moment up than it relinquishes it to the emptiness of the present: 'I read, much of the night, and go south in the winter'.

So these, we might feel, taking our cue from the poem's title, are the dead who are to be buried, and it is their failures which are denounced by the prophetic voice instantly raised against them.

> What are the roots that clutch, what branches grow
> Out of this stony rubbish? Son of man,
> You cannot say, or guess, for you know only
> A heap of broken images, where the sun beats,
> And the dead tree gives no shelter, the cricket no relief . . .

But Marie is clearly not stony rubbish. This booming prophet is no answer to the pathos of her words; on the contrary, it is his denunciations which make a desert out of the images that have gone before, giving no shelter, no relief, but beating down remorselessly to reduce the world to dust. His condemnation, like his invitation, insidiously folded into the apparent aside of a parenthesis '(Come in under the shadow of this red rock)', is deathly, the first of many refusals to hear the voices of women.[16]

For their voices are crucial. If recent decades of literary criticism have taught us anything, they will have helped us to read *The Waste Land* as a gendered drama moved by those interactions between men and women which constitute its declared or secret text. It is Marie who provokes the fear-wielding prophet with his shadows and handful of dust; it is the girl in the hyacinth-garden who is placed at the centre of 'Burial of the Dead', and words from *Tristan and Isolde* overarch the episode on either side.

Eliot's Notes to the poem (published as an integral part of the work since 1922) are careful to point to exact junctures of the Tristan story—not the ecstasy of love or its transcendence of death, both of which are amply evoked by Wagner's opera, but more disturbing realizations: the moment when love is recognized as peril; the moment when desolation is embraced. '*Frisch weht der Wind . . . Oed' und leer das Meer*'. The lines have their own music and summon up Wagner's too, but as though his romantic tragedy has only emptiness at its heart. And between this beginning and end (an end which the opera as a whole would endeavour to deny) comes the uncomplaining voice of the girl who knows both who she was and who she is no longer:

> 'You gave me hyacinths first a year ago;
> 'They called me the hyacinth girl.'

That, in its unillusioned acceptance of the past tense, is without bitterness, though sad. It is the man who is still trapped within the experience of passion, unable to understand. He is the one compelled into speech, needing to answer her finished sentence with a '—Yet', a different view, only to find himself silenced, entranced, taken out of life, but whether into ecstasy or annulment who can say?

—Yet when we came back, late, from the hyacinth garden,
Your arms full, and your hair wet, I could not
Speak, and my eyes failed, I was neither
Living nor dead, and I knew nothing,
Looking into the heart of light, the silence.

That final moment is an enigma, impossible to translate. If it is followed immediately by '*Oed' und leer das Meer*', those words are in another voice, another language, and simplify the experience which the poetry itself has kept before us mysteriously ambivalent and unreduced. The heart of light, the silence, remains the point at which both speech and vision fail; sightless, wordless, neither living nor dead, one can say only—the poetry says exactly—that in this moment one knows 'nothing'.

That is, however, in Eliot's view a great thing to have known. The abyss into which one cannot peer, but where intensity of life is gathered: this is no simple negative, though negatives alone declare it: 'not . . . neither . . . nothing . . . silence', rhyming (as it were) across four lines with 'hyacinth garden', after which the episode, enclosed by Wagner at its start and finish, is ended by another nothing, the blank white of empty space between the paragraphs on the page. Being neither life nor death, this experience which brings us to know 'nothing' as we have not known it before is inscrutable. Only from the midst of it the woman's voice, '"They called me the hyacinth girl"', remains.

The poem answers her with another woman. Madame Sosostris is spoken into existence unforgettably ('Had a bad cold, nevertheless': what deft prestigidation, what use of the *vers-libre* line to unfold a statement only to whisk it out of sight); more to the point, however, she has her own voice, and the first thing it does is summon up the drama's hidden end. Creepy, predatory, ridiculous with her wicked pack of cards, she is ('nevertheless') no simple fraud. At least, she has more to show than the desert prophet had.

Here, said she,
Is your card, the drowned Phoenician Sailor,
(Those are pearls that were his eyes. Look!)

That transformation of the lifeless body into beauty is something deep, unfathomable; but the even more astonishing fact is that it is 'your' card on which this destiny is written, relating Phlebas's death by water to the moment in the hyacinth garden where a You looked into the heart of light and could not answer the girl with her arms full of flowers. The glimpse is allowed, then lost. For mostly, of course, the practices of the fortune-teller debase whatever they touch; her ominous mutterings parody understanding, and her blank card 'Which I am forbidden to see' is hardly a reproduction of the void into which we cannot peer. Yet it is she who, pointing to the drowned Phoenician Sailor, enables us to bring together experiences otherwise far apart—'Here . . . Is your card', 'Look!'. So we may realize, looking to the pattern, that whereas the abyss in the garden left vision immobilized and desire unable to move, the impasse of that revelation is not the end. In a death by water which need not be feared, the abyss of the whirlpool will carry the body of the dead life out of the world forever.

Entering the whirlpool

It is an irony structural to 'The Burial of the Dead' that its dead cannot be buried. The crowds walk round in a ring, flow over London Bridge and up the hill to where the church clock having spoken the hour moves onwards, preparing to strike its dead note yet again. Or he who was with you in the ships at Mylae reappears. Or roots clutch, branches grow, April stirs the land to life once more. There is no finality here. Which is no doubt why the poem finishes where Baudelaire's *Fleurs du Mal began,*[17] with a vision of reader and poet gazing into each other's eyes, both of them bedevilled and sinful yet somehow bored to death—

> 'You! hypocrite lecteur!—mon semblable,—mon frère!'

—not an end but a mock-end, the stasis of utter ennui and inertia, a parody of the stillness in the hyacinth garden, a parody of death and yet quite deadly enough. The second movement of *The Waste Land* makes a new approach.

Magnificent, ornamental, drawing on the richest period of English drama, the opening lines rewrite Cleopatra's scene of triumph as she sails down river to capture Antony's heart: 'The

Barge she sat in, like a burnisht Throne/Burnt on the water' (*Antony and Cleopatra*, II. ii). In Shakespeare's pageant, everything is living movement: the winds, the oars, the fans that glow more beauty into Cleopatra's cheek, the children and servingmaids who seem like nereids and cupids as they tend her. In 'A Game of Chess'—title taken from another Jacobean play—there is movement still, but 'strange, synthetic', troublingly artificial, as the glitter of jewels rises to meet redoubled candleflames, and perfumes confuse and drown the sense in odours. The syntax itself is disorientingly alive, inviting one reading of a line only to allow another, or changing passive into active under our gaze. Each item reflects some other, the glass itself, 'Held up by standards wrought with fruited vines', reflecting the mirror on Belinda's dressing-table in *The Rape of the Lock*, and Lamia's banquet-hall in a poem by Keats, at the same time as it holds a profane resemblance—'From which a golden Cupidon peeped out/(Another hid his eyes behind his wing)'—to the splendour Isaiah's cherubim dared not look upon.

So the scene refuses to resolve itself into a straightforward understanding. If stories of Woman as seductress and betrayer stir to life in the allusions of the verse, so too do the tales of women deserted and betrayed: Dido abandoned by Aeneas, Philomela raped by her brother-in-law, Eve preyed on by Satan, or Imogen by Iachimo. On every side are wrongs, and the poetry arrives at no simple moral, any more than it simply parodies or degrades the past in taking up Shakespeare, Marlowe and all the other authors it twists and refashions. What is produced is something new, intense and disturbing. For the past is full of horrors, however distanced and transformed; even its beauty now is embroidered into withered stumps, staring forms that lean out, leaning, swelling through the surface and around the 'room enclosed', so that the two speakers who begin at line 111 are already surrounded by evidences of the pain men and women can inflict on one another.

> 'My nerves are bad tonight. Yes, bad. Stay with me.
> 'Speak to me. Why do you never speak. Speak.'
> 'What are you thinking of? What thinking? What?
> 'I never know what you are thinking. Think.'

It is, or used to be, a commonplace of criticism to describe the woman as a neurasthenic—which puts her in a category of the abnormal and justifies her companion's holding aloof.[18] But the response her words provoke from him (do we know the other speaker is male?) is not a holding off, so much as a fatigued, cold cruelty of the mind. To her desperate rushes of demand and attack, 'he' replies with a vision as disordered as her own: 'I think we are in rats' alley/Where the dead men lost their bones'. Little enough that's human there. Wearied, pitiless, the responses greet her desperation as 'Nothing again nothing', or answer only by turning away: 'Those are pearls that were his eyes', or 'O O O O that Shakespeherian Rag'[19]: another snatch of music from another time to distract from the sound of her voice, until her final threat to '"rush out as I am, and walk the street/With my hair down, so"' is overmastered by the far more sinister closure her interlocutor provides:

And we shall play a game of chess,
Pressing lidless eyes and waiting for a knock upon the door

(with its echo of *Women Beware Women*, Jacobean tragedy of multiple betrayals).[20] If this is the last word between those speakers, the pub scene comes as a relief.

It is strange that it should seem so, when the misery of Lil and Albert's story is made so much worse by the relish with which the speaker tells it. She—Lil's friend and confidante—has her own line in heartlessness, matching the voice which says we are in rats' alley. She likewise is determined not to hear or feel or give: 'I didn't mince my words . . . If you don't like it you can get on with it, I said. . . . What you get married for if you don't want children?' Women Beware Women indeed. And yet, even in depicting her calloused manipulations the poetry does not sneer or simply condemn. Instead, her shrunken life, and Lil's, and Albert's are all caught up in what we gradually hear as a rhythm of the desperate, brightly knowing post-war years when husbands are 'demobbed' (verb of 1919, first recorded 1920) and all the modern ways prevail. 'If you don't give it him, there's others will, I said. . . . Then I'll know who to thank, she said, and give me a straight look. . . . It's them pills I took to bring it off, she said. . . . You ought to be ashamed, I said, to look so antique.' *She said, I said*: in their stylized pattern the words move like a dance-step, foxtrot- or charleston-fashion.

> You *are* a proper fool, I said.
> Well, if Albert won't leave you alone, there it is, I said

A dance, but also a tic douloureux: the effect is particularly poignant in the recordings Eliot himself made of the scene, where his voice renders its tunes with such deliberate sad syncopations, such trapped vivacity of emphasis. These lives are not dismissed as worthless, or gazed on blankly from outside; men and women alike, they take their place in a dance to the music of time, and Ophelia's farewell as it blends with the air of ragtime ('Good night, ladies  good night, sweet ladies, good night, good night') provides the benediction they cannot think of for themselves. Her words reach back even to that over-ornate room where demand and refusal were locked together ('"Are you alive, or not? Is there nothing in your head?"'), and with gentle unself-pitying pity leave the figures in 'A Game of Chess' at peace.

But the fountain sprang up and the bird sang down

Why Ophelia? Perhaps just because she is one of those whom fathers and brothers, suitors, rulers—the male formations—fail to hear. Persuaded into love by Hamlet, she is discarded and forced to disown the assurances she was given: 'I was the more deceived'. Yet it is her voice which outlasts the admonitions of the doomsday-speaking barman: 'HURRY UP PLEASE ITS TIME'; and it is her fate, like Phlebas, to be repossessed by nature ('mermaid-like a while', says Gertrude) in a hauntingly ambiguous end. To listen to Ophelia and *The Waste Land*'s other voices of women, then, is precisely not to participate in what Alison Tate identifies as a privileging of male discourse in the poem. For Tate, the 'serious, authoritative discourses of the poem', its prophetic voices and impersonal effects, are 'aligned with the masculine', while its women, excluded or treated voyeuristically by the realm of the high-literary, are vernacularized and degraded; they speak inconsequentially, 'they are garrulous, they chatter', she declares.

> The poem can be seen to replicate in its structure . . . the history of inclusions and exclusions of the English literary tradition. In

> the hierarchies set up within *The Waste Land*, the excluded, the subordinated terms, are those representing women, the working class, speech and dialect.
>
> ('The Master-Narrative of Modernism: Discourses of Gender and Class in *The Waste Land*', p. 160; see also pp. 162, 164)

It will be clear by now that my own reading of the poem is almost the opposite. The bringer of fear in a handful of dust, the I who in the presence of the hyacinth-girl can neither speak nor see, or the one who in the presence of the suffering woman with her nerves and outbursts thinks we are in rats' alley—none of these is 'authoritative' in my view, and though they might claim supremacy over the life of the pub or other 'feminine' discourses of the poem, the poetry itself does not allow their claims. *Its* centre is music of just the kind they never reach:

> yet there the nightingale
> Filled all the desert with inviolable voice

—and desert and nightingale confront one another inescapably in the Tiresias episode, midway through that Fire Sermon which itself comes at the mid point of the poem.

To Tiresias, everything is known already, and all of it is observed without pity. In his own eyes, even he is just one more item coldly scrutinized—'old man with wrinkled dugs'—as though alien if not repellent to himself. Under his remorseless gaze, the typist is placed amid the makeshifts of her lodgings—

> On the divan are piled (at night her bed)
> Stockings, slippers, camisoles, and stays—

and the same gaze finds out the small house-agent's clerk as 'One of the low on whom assurance sits/As a silk hat on a Bradford millionaire'. All do offend; food in tins, exploring hands, the human engine like a taxi: contemptuous, and yet indifferent, Tiresias' seeing is 'the dead heart of *The Waste Land*' (A. D. Moody, 1979, p. 92).

We are not left to experience it on its own terms, though. Instead, the Seer's seeing of these lives is surrounded and broken in upon by lyrical powers not at his command, so that the Tiresias-vision is known for what it is: a sort of blindness.

At the violet hour, when the eyes and back
Turn upward from the desk, when the human engine waits
Like a taxi throbbing waiting,
I Tiresias, though blind, throbbing between two lives,
Old man with wrinkled female breasts, can see
At the violet hour, the evening hour that strives
Homeward, and brings the sailor home from sea,
The typist home at teatime, clears her breakfast, lights
Her stove, and lays out food in tins.

Twice the verse summons up that transfiguring moment 'At the violet hour', and twice it starts out in one direction only to be waylaid and diverted into another, in defiance of Tiresias, as it were. Sappho sang of Hesperus the evening star 'herding homewards all that shining Dawn had sent abroad'; here, the evening hour unfolds its reconciliation within the onward movement of the sentence, to bring the typist like the sailor home and lend an unlooked-for beauty to the scene. It might almost be called heroic. Out of the window perilously spread hang 'combinations' magically unsupported by the grammar, yet touched into grandeur by the phrasing—touched by tenderness too. The casements of 'Ode to a Nightingale' also opened upon that haunting adjective 'perilous'; and now that we think of nightingales, we might remember how we met them before in Sweeney's company (p. 36 above). So the sexual encounter climaxing the scene is predictable enough; what could not have been foretold is the epic resonance with which it is invested. Yet rhythm and vocabulary dignify it, as when in *carbuncular* (a carbuncle is a precious stone, as well as a boil-like infection), or *propitious, engage, defence, enact, bestow*, Tiresias' cold stare falling on the action is mysteriously turned into an occasion of splendour instead. The degradation of the assault is not forgotten, but neither is it just confirmed; in the poetry it is seen and felt in a perspective so much larger than Tiresias' that, when everything is over, the summation offered by lyric, '"This music crept by me upon the waters"', may seem movingly appropriate after all.

At all events, it is not simply mocking or reductive. 'This music' may be the gramophone's automatic answer to what has gone before, but it is the music of the typist's own voice, too, as she acknowledges herself in the mirror, '"Well now that's done: and I'm glad it's over"'. Music presents her and at the same time misses her plight, 'When lovely woman stoops to folly', in phrases drawn from an eighteenth-century song; and the strains which creep by us upon the waters are like those which Ferdinand hears, in *The Tempest* (I. ii. 390), calming his grief at the supposed death of his father—the effect encompasses all these together. When 'The Fire Sermon' opened, death was grotesque and fearsome to the mind, and so indeed was sex:

> White bodies naked on the low damp ground
> And bones cast in a little low dry garret,
> Rattled by the rat's foot only, year to year

But as a kind of Ariel music, simultaneously leading and pursuing, carries the poetry 'along the Strand, up Queen Victoria Street', London ceases to be a place of horrors, and becomes instead an object both of lamentation and delight ('O City city'). A mandoline's pleasant whining and the clatter and the chatter of a public bar can be held in the same imaginative embrace as Magnus Martyr's white and gold; there is nothing to be recoiled from here. Likewise with the oil and tar the river sweats, the barges and docklands of the busy unbeautiful Isle of Dogs, or the gilded shell of Elizabeth and Leicester's barque: the mind sees past and present, mess and magnificence together, and combines them into lyric, not using the one to denigrate the other. At last, even the three Thames daughters uttering their stories can be accepted uncondemned, dire though the condition is into which they have been brought.

> 'Trams and dusty trees.
> Highbury bore me. Richmond and Kew
> Undid me. By Richmond I raised my knees
> Supine on the floor of a narrow canoe.'

In turn, each speaks her own account of final destitution, her song of sex *as* death. The experience is held steadily before the mind, without illusion but without bitterness either. This is what human relations may come to.

'. . .
I can connect
Nothing with nothing.
The broken fingernails of dirty hands.
My people humble people who expect
Nothing.'

It is pain and numbness both together, the end of hope, the emptying out of life. And yet precisely here, where destitution is known for what it is, the poem has the power and will to begin anew. Saint Augustine had written 'To Carthage then I came, where a cauldron of unholy loves sang all about mine ears'. The Thames daughters speak from the ashes; but as they do, from Richmond and Kew eastwards to Moorgate and on to the estuary at Margate where the river enters the sea, the poem travels towards its transformational death by water, where unredeemed living is ended and laid aside.

No one will think that is easy. With 'The Fire Sermon''s burning away of human desire, the conditions upon which renewal must be based, if it is to be gained at all, are revealed as dreadful: they mean the death of all we ordinarily understand by life, and the final movement of *The Waste Land* begins in nightmare, as though whatever moment of peace was glimpsed in the passing of Phlebas the Phoenician cannot be relied on, but must be sought and lost and reached for time and again.

So the last phase of the poem starts. 'After the torchlight red on sweaty faces', after the tumults of the opening of 'What the Thunder Said', what is left are the old words *dead* and *dying*, but in a subtly changed pattern now:

He who was living is now dead
We who were living are now dying
With a little patience

—the final term echoes back across the lines, its resonance not even closed by punctuation (there is no full-stop). And 'patience' might be the word for the quiet persistence that holds on through the reiterated nightmare of rock and sand, until the 'Dead mountain mouth of carious teeth that cannot spit' gives way to a different visionary landscape, something won from the very *absence* of relief:

If there were water
And no rock
If there were rock
And also water
And water
A spring
A pool among the rock
If there were the sound of water only
Not the cicada
And dry grass singing
But sound of water over a rock
Where the hermit-thrush sings in the pine trees
Drip drop drip drop drop drop drop
But there is no water

Only by attending to the lines' delicate movement, their quiet stepping from rock to rock, can one tell the difference the poetry seeks to establish between dream and mere mirage. The mind is not deluded—'there is no water' in fact—but it is momentarily blessed in the imagined water's singing of itself. And in this new condition the dreamlike presence of another, that 'third who walks always beside you . . . wrapt in a brown mantle', can be welcomed and greeted, whether man or woman, without revulsion or fear. The pitiless heaps of the desert, the suffocating 'room enclosed', or the rat-trodden vegetation by the dull canal where Ferdinand mused on death: all these are left behind. Nightmare landscapes and disintegrating cities, Vienna, London, have become in a word 'Unreal'; and even sexualized terrors ('A woman drew her long black hair out tight') subside into reminiscent bells and voices singing.

Everything is empty at this site the poem has reached—the chapel, the cisterns and wells; but instead of the 'nothing' into which the poem gazed speechless and sightless in the hyacinth garden, absence here is filled with life. Once, there was the heart of light, the silence, a plenitude never to be embraced; now, in this decayed hole among the mountains, the grass is singing, the graves are tumbled as if by sleepers stirring awake, and the very vacancy of the chapel gives the wind its 'home'. Then a flash of lightning, and 'a damp gust/Bringing rain'.

Where is the end of them . . . ?

How much simpler, less demanding on the reader, to have climaxed the poem with a choric proclamation of fertility restored to some allegorical desert. But that is not how *The Waste Land* ends. Instead, there are 'fragments . . . shored against my ruins' and a glimpse of the arid plain and of falling London and *la tour abolie*. If some voices can be heard intoning 'Shantih shantih shantih' ('"The Peace which passeth understanding" is a feeble translation of the content of this word', said Eliot's original Note), others cry out of Purgatory or their hell of desolation. '*Poi s'ascose nel foco* . . . Hieronymo's mad againe'. It is not even that, as F. R. Leavis judged, 'The poem exhibits no progression . . . and ends where it began' (*New Bearings*, p. 103); more complicatedly, it speaks against itself, and against attempts to draw it into unity and single-hearted resolution. It will not even let us regard it as an aesthetic document from which as readers we can safely turn away. Maddened Hieronymo's snarl, 'Why then Ile fit you', is a vengeful *warning* to those who hear him, that he will bring down their world.

We are hardly used to poems actually meaning what they say, but the scene in *The Spanish Tragedy* (IV. i) to which Eliot's closing lines allude casts its own weird light on *The Waste Land*'s enterprise. Hieronymo has shown his enemies a book: 'It was my chance to write a tragedie', he says;

> Now would your Lordships favour me so much
> As but to grace mee with your acting it—
> I mean each one of you to play a part—
> Assure you, it will proove most passing strange

For one thing, it will result in the actors being killed in earnest; but even before that, 'Each one of us/Must act his part in unknown languages', as Hieronymo himself does, before, in a last defiance, he bites his own tongue out and spits it at the King.

It has been the argument of this study that the reader of Eliot's verse likewise 'Must act his part in unknown languages', experiencing—as one's own experience—a text which would implicate our consciousness in its: Words echoing 'Thus, in your mind' make us co-workers. So, 'You! hypocrite lecteur!—mon semblable,—mon frère!', says the last line of 'The Burial of the Dead' in the voice of a dead author in a different poem in another language inside Eliot's own . . . except that *The Waste Land* makes it impossible to decide what language *is* its author's 'own', or even where the 'author' begins and ends, or who/what might be thus addressed by this simultaneity, BaudelaireEliotLanguage, and named so confidently 'You'. Hypocrite lecteur: at best, perhaps, we could conclude that 'he' (we) will always be ourselves, and always equally not-self, a merely formal sign, of otherness elsewhere.

I don't read *The Waste Land*, therefore, as a poem about its author any more than I read it as a poem about Western Civilization (say). Around all those terms—*I, poem, author, civilization*, not to mention the would-be referential prepositions *about, around*—chasms have opened in recent years. In proposing that *The Waste Land* is a poem 'about' or 'of' its readers, I assume no firm ground whatever underfoot; merely, the chance of a different reading: that the states of consciousness dramatized throughout are 'your' consciousness, reader, as you read, and the seemingly other-person figures—*me, she*, and all the rest—are incidents or happenings within it.

> Then spoke the thunder
> Da
> *Datta:* what have we given?
> My friend, blood shaking my heart
> The awful daring of a moment's surrender
> Which an age of prudence can never retract
> By this, and this only, we have existed

The shift from one pronoun to another, 'me' to 'we', epitomizes the process. But so too does the shift from the thunder's language-exceeding, prelinguistic Da, to the first interpretation of it, as '*Datta*': *Give*, and then its further interpretation into particularities which belong both to individual and to common life—whereby the unique moment of surrender, known only in 'my' heart, is absorbed and vanishes into the universal process of 'memories draped by the beneficent spider', or the silence we leave behind in 'our empty rooms'.

If it were not for the possibility of *mine* becoming *ours* in some such way, consciousness would be a stronghold locked upon itself, sustained only by devouring its own products.

> I have heard the key
> Turn in the door once and turn once only

Dante's Ugolino had been left to starve in a tower where there was nothing to eat but his own flesh or his children's. The Note to line 411 refers us to that hideousness (*Inferno*, xxxiii), but also to the subject of Eliot's own doctoral dissertation for Harvard (1911–16), the philosopher F. H. Bradley, who had proposed: 'all experience falls within my own circle, a circle closed on the outside; and . . . every sphere is opaque to the others which surround it'. However arrived at, the prison of the self is Hell, and if, under the sign of *Dayadhvam: Sympathize*, ethereal rumours promise some release, it is only 'for a moment', and only a 'broken Coriolanus', a self dead to its former life, that might conceivably revive. Otherwise, 'each in his prison/Thinking of the key, each confirms a prison'.

And so the thunder speaks its last word, identical with its first and with all it will ever say, but now reinterpreted and newly understood:

> DA
> *Damyata:* The boat responded
> Gaily, to the hand expert with sail and oar
> The sea was calm, your heart would have responded
> Gaily, when invited, beating obedient
> To controlling hands

Of all words to find at the end of this poem, 'Gaily' (twice) is one we would never expect. The easy joy and freedom of the boat on the sea is a natural thing, and yet dependent on skill. So likewise with love, the imagery seems to say—except that, for human beings, uncertainty, resistance, conditionality, inevitably enter in; 'your heart would have responded/Gaily', but didn't. That achieved happiness is not in the poem. But then, neither is any human being in fact. When the lines address themselves to 'your' heart, the poet, the reader, some other imagined third person, are all present as possibilities in the pronoun, but actual life in the world of choice and action must go on elsewhere. So the writing evokes a vision of fulfilment and, simultaneously, the knowledge of its absence: a failure, something missed and lost. After all, the heart will not beat obedient to controlling hands just because a poem says so; rather, for Hieronymo's strategy to take effect, the imaginary world of art must breach its boundaries and turn into action instead: real live action—which means, in Hieronymo's tragedy, real deadly death-bringing deeds.

A kind of dying is what you are to practise, says *The Waste Land*, if 'your' heart is to respond and make actual the fulfilment which in the poem is unattained and missed. This is a hard doctrine, but the reader is offered it all the same. Ophelia, the hyacinth girl, the music of sensual life that 'crept by me upon the waters': all the poetry's figures and voices of beauty have been evoked, not that they may be desired, but that they may be transcended. And if transcendence sometimes seems too easy—as with Jerusalem, Athens, Alexandria summoned up in dismissal as 'Unreal'—the poem's final movement poignantly declares what it yearns for, and acknowledges the cost. The thunder is made to speak the awful daring of a moment's surrender; the aethereal rumours only a broken Coriolanus will hear; the heart whose joy is not in itself but in beating obedient to controlling hands. Even its moments of peace, like the water-dripping song of the hermit-thrush, or the vacant chapel where the door swings, are centred on what is not there, but promised and found (if at all) beyond. The result is a sort of dying to the ordinary world.

'Dry bones can harm no one.' With all the resources of a great poet, *The Waste Land* urges the reader to pass into the nothingness of that, and make it real. So the soul in Purgatory plunges back in the fire that refines it—'*Poi s'ascose nel foco che gli affina*'—but only it can choose to hasten its deliverance this way. On this reading, purgatorial is what *The Waste Land* is. By being so conscious of its work as poetry ('My words echo/Thus, in your mind'), it would make us conscious of all that poetry cannot do, and must leave to lived choice and action in its reader instead.

NOTES

1 *Making It All Up*

1 Examples in the opening pages of Hugh Kenner's *The Invisible Poet* (New York: Citadel), 1964 , and F. R. Leavis, 'Approaches to T. S. Eliot', in *The Common Pursuit* (London: Chatto & Windus), 1958. The puzzled reader in the 1950s was myself, in a first-year tutorial. Commentators who did not realize they were dealing with a poem are discussed by Donald Davie, 'Pound and Eliot: a distinction', in Graham Martin, ed., *Eliot in Perspective* (London: Macmillan), 1970, pp. 75–82.

2 'If I believed that my reply would be to one who would ever return to earth, this flame would be forever still; but since no one has ever returned alive from this gulf, if what I hear is true, I can answer you without fear of infamy.'

3 O *quam te memoram virgo*: the half-line from Virgil's *Aeneid* might be rendered as, 'O maiden, how shall I speak of you?'.

2 *Replacings*

4 See Peter Ackroyd, *T. S. Eliot* (London: Hamish Hamilton) 1984; Lyndall Gordon, 1977, and also her *Eliot's New Life* (Oxford: OUP), 1988. Another way of creating biography is offered by A. D. Moody, 1979, pp. 1–13.

5 *The Egoist*, IV. ii. (December 1917), p. 167.

6 *The Paris Review*, reprinted in Van Wyck Brooks, ed., *Writers at Work*, second series (London: Secker & Warburg), 1963, p. 70. The next two quotations come from 'The Eliot Family and St. Louis', *Washington University Studies*, new series, no. 23, pp. 28–9, and Eliot's Preface to Edgar A. Mowrer, *This American World* (New York: Houghton Mifflin), 1928.

7 *Poems Written in Early Youth* (London: Faber) were first published 1967; from 1969 they have been included in the *Complete Poems and Plays*.

8 See, for example, Elizabeth Drew, *T. S. Eliot: the Design of his Poetry* (New York: Scribner), 1949, p. 47: 'Like Mr Prufrock, he lays bare his psychological dilemma . . .'

9 Words from the recurrent Chorus of Angels in *The Dream of Gerontius*, later adapted as hymn 471 of *The English Hymnal*, 'Praise to the Holiest in the Height'.

10 'It was like a sudden conversion', wrote Eliot of his first encounter with Fitzgerald's translation; 'the world appeared anew, painted with bright, delicious and painful colours. Thereupon I took the usual adolescent course with Byron, Shelley, Keats, Rossetti, Swinburne' (*The Use of Poetry and the Use of Criticism*, p. 33).

11 The Blessed Damozel, in Dante Gabriel Rossetti's poem of that name, imagines the arrival in heaven of her earthly love:

> We two will lie i' the shadow of
>   That living mystic tree
> Within whose secret growth the Dove
>   Is sometimes felt to be,
> While every leaf that His plumes touch
>   Saith His Name audibly.
> (stanza 16)

3 *In Different Voices*

12 These remarks in 'The Music of Poetry' (*On Poetry and Poets*, p. 37), and the just-quoted passage on rhythm bringing to birth the idea and the image, might be compared with Eliot's description of *The Waste Land* as 'a piece of rhythmical

grumbling' (quoted in Valerie Eliot, ed., *The Waste Land: A facsimile and transcript of the original drafts*, p. 1; or with the letter from Eliot's eldest sister (quoted as an epigraph to Valerie Eliot, ed., *The Letters of T. S. Eliot*, vol. 1, 1898–1922 (London: Faber), 1988, p. xxxi).

> When you were a tiny boy, learning to talk, you used to sound the rhythm of sentences without shaping words—the ups and downs of the thing you were trying to say. I used to answer you in kind, saying nothing and yet conversing with you as we sat side by side on the stairs at 2635 Locust Street. And now you think the rhythm before the words in a new poem! . . . Such a dear little boy!

13 These observations, and other materials relevant to the history of *The Waste Land*, are in D. D. Paige, ed., *The Letters of Ezra Pound* (London: Faber), 1951, pp. 234 ff. Pound's letter of 24 December 1921 also printed in *The Letters of T. S. Eliot*, pp. 497–8.

14 *Paris Review* interview, Van Wyck Brooks, *op. cit.*, p. 83.

15 See, for example, versions of 'Dirge' printed in *The Waste Land: a facsimile and transcript* . . ., p. 118–23:

> Full fathom five your Bleistein lies
> Under the flatfish and the squids
> Grave's Disease in a dead jew's eyes!
> When the crabs have eat the lids.
> Lower than the wharf rats dive
> Though he suffer a sea-change
> Still expensive rich and strange. . . .

16 This particular parenthesis is illuminatingly examined by Christopher Ricks in his *T. S. Eliot and Prejudice* (London: Faber), 1988, pp. 152–3.

17 The opening poem, 'Au Lecteur', is given in French and English in Marthiel and Jackson Mathews, *Charles Baudelaire:* The Flowers of Evil (London: Routledge), 1955; Roy Campbell's translation, pp. 3–4, concludes:

> In each man's foul menagerie of sin
>
> There's one more damned than all. He never gambols
> Nor crawls, nor roars, but, from the rest withdrawn,

Gladly of this whole earth would make a shambles
And swallow up existence with a yawn . . .

Boredom! He smokes his hookah, while he dreams
Of gibbets, weeping tears he cannot smother.
You know this dainty monster, too, it seems—
Hypocrite reader!—You!—my twin!—My brother!

18 The term neurasthenic (meaning *nervous debility* or *liability to hysteria*) was helped on its way by being used in one of the earliest analytical investigations of the poem: F. R. Leavis, *New Bearings in English Poetry* (London: Chatto and Windus), first published 1932.

19 'Roy Samuel's big hit in *Ziegfield's Follies* of 1912', according to the publishers of the sheet music. Words were by Gene Buck and Herman Ruby, music by David Stamper, and the chorus begins:

That Shakespearian rag
Most intelligent, very elegant,
That old classical drag,
Has the proper stuff. . . .

20 The relevant portion of the plot is neatly summarized in B.C. Southam, *A Student's Guide to the Selected Poems*, p. 79.

FURTHER READING

Works by T. S. Eliot

The Complete Poems and Plays (London: Faber), 1969.
Selected Essays (London: Faber), 1932, rev. ed. 1953.
On Poetry and Poets (London: Faber), 1957.
The Use of Poetry and the Use of Criticism (London: Faber), 1933.
ed. Valerie Eliot, *The Waste Land: a facsimile and transcript of the original drafts, including the annotations of Ezra Pound* (London: Faber), 1971.

Additional material

Bedient, Calvin, *He Do the Police in Different Voices:* The Waste Land *and its Protagonist*, (Chicago: UCP), 1986.
Gordon, Lyndall, *Eliot's Early Years* (Oxford: OUP), 1977.
Kenner, Hugh, *The Invisible Poet: T. S. Eliot* (New York: Ivan Obolensky), 1959.
ed., *T. S. Eliot: a collection of critical essays*, Twentieth-Century Views, (Eaglewood Cliffs, N. J.: Prentice-Hall), 1962.
Leavis, F. R., *New Bearings in English Poetry* (London: Chatto and Windus), 1932.

Martin, Graham, ed., *Eliot in Perspective* (London: Macmillan), 1970.
Moody, A. D., *Thomas Stearns Eliot: Poet* (Cambridge: CUP), 1979.
ed., The Waste Land *in Different Voices* (London: Edward Arnold), 1974.
ed., *The Cambridge Companion to T. S. Eliot* (Cambridge: CUP), 1993.
Olney, James, ed., *T. S. Eliot: Essays from the* Southern Review (Oxford: Clarendon Press), 1988.
Ricks, Christopher, *T. S. Eliot and Prejudice* (London: Faber), 1988.
Southam, B. C., *A Student's Guide to the Selected Poems of T. S. Eliot* (London: Faber), 1968.
Tate, Alison, 'The Master-Narrative of Modernism: Discourses of Gender and Class in *The Waste Land*', *Literature and History*, 14: 2, Autumn, 1988, pp. 160–71.